# Venice

## DIRECTIONS

WRITTEN AND RESEARCHED BY

## Jonathan Buckley

**ROUGH GUIDES**

NEW YORK • LONDON • DELHI

www.roughguides.com

# Contents

# Introduction to

# Venice

*Founded 1500 years ago on a cluster of mudflats in the centre of the lagoon, Venice rose to become Europe's main trading post between the West and the East, and at its height controlled an empire that extended from the Dolomites to Cyprus. The melancholic air of the place is in part a product of the discrepancy between the grandeur of its history and what the city has become.*

In the heyday of the Venetian Republic, some 200,000 people lived in Venice, three times its present population. Merchants from Europe and western Asia maintained warehouses here; transactions in the banks and bazaars of the

Rialto dictated the value of commodities all over the continent; in the dockyards of the Arsenale the workforce was so vast that a warship could be built and fitted out in a single day; and the Piazza San Marco was thronged with people here to set up deals or report to the Republic's government. Nowadays it's no longer a buzzing metropolis but rather the embodiment of a fabulous past, dependent for its survival largely on the people who come to marvel at its relics.

The monuments which draw the largest crowds are the Basilica di San Marco – the mausoleum of the city's patron saint – and the Palazzo Ducale or Doge's

▲ A Cannaregio canal view

Palace. Certainly these are the most imposing structures in the city, but a roll-call of the churches worth visiting would feature more than a dozen names. Many of the city's treasures remain in the churches for which they were created, but a sizeable number have been removed to one or other of Venice's museums, with the Accademia holding the lion's share. This cultural heritage is a source of endless fascination, but you should also discard your itineraries for a day and just wander – the anonymous parts of Venice reveal as much of the city as its well-known attractions.

▼ The Piazzetta

## When to visit

Venice's tourist season is very nearly an all-year affair. Peak season, when hotel rooms are virtually impossible to come by at short notice, is from **April to October**; try to avoid **July and August** in particular, when the climate becomes oppressively hot and clammy. The other two popular spells are the **Carnevale** (leading up to Lent) and the weeks on each side of **Christmas**. For the ideal combination of comparative peace and a mild climate, the two or three weeks **immediately preceding Easter** is perhaps the best time of year. Climatically the months at the end of the high season are somewhat less reliable: some **November and December** days bring fogs that make it difficult to see from one bank of the Canal Grande to the other. If you want to see the city at its quietest, **January** is the month to go – take plenty of warm clothes, though, as the winds of the Adriatic can be savage, and you should be prepared for floods throughout the winter. This **acqua alta**, as Venice's seasonal flooding is called, has been an element of Venetian life for centuries, but nowadays it's far more frequent than it used to be: between October and late February it's not uncommon for flooding to occur every day of the week, and it'll be a long time before the huge flood barrier (which was begun in 2003) makes any impact. However, having lived with it for so long, the city is well geared to dealing with the nuisance. Shopkeepers in the most badly affected areas insert steel shutters into their doorways to hold the water at bay, while the local council lays jetties of duck-boards along the major thoroughfares and between the chief vaporetto stops and dry land.

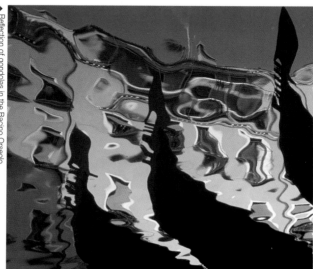

► Reflection of gondolas in the Bacino Orseolo

## ›› VENICE AT A GLANCE

The historic centre of Venice is made up of 118 islands, tied together by some 400 bridges to form an amalgamation that's divided into six large administrative districts known as sestieri, three on each side of the Canal Grande.

### San Marco

The sestiere of San Marco is the hub of the city, being the location of the two prime monuments – the Palazzo Ducale and the Basilica di San Marco – and the city's highest concentration of shops and hotels.

▲ The Basilica di San Marco

▲ The San Barnaba district

### Castello

Spreading north and east of San Marco, the sprawling sestiere of Castello encompasses many of Venice's most interesting churches, its former industrial centre, and some of its grittier residential areas.

### Dorsoduro

Lying on the opposite side of the Canal Grande from San Marco, and stretching westward to the docks, Dorsoduro is one of the city's smartest quarters, as well as the home of its university and the main art gallery.

▲ San Pietro di Castello

◄ Murano

### San Polo and Santa Croce

Adjoining Dorsoduro to the north, the sestieri of San Polo and Santa Croce are riddled with intricate alleyways and characterful little squares – and it's here that you'll find the famous Rialto market.

### Northern islands

The nearest of the northern islands of the lagoon – San Michele – is the city's historic cemetery; a little farther out lies the glassmaking island of Murano, while in the outermost reaches you'll find Burano and Torcello, Venice's predecessor.

### Southern islands

Sheltered from the Adriatic by the Lido and its neighbouring sandbanks, the southern part of the lagoon has a scattering of islands, notably San Giorgio Maggiore and La Giudecca, the focus of some major redevelopment projects.

◄ Campo San Polo

### Cannaregio

The train station occupies a corner of Cannaregio, and most of the city's one-star hotels are clustered nearby, but much of this district is tranquil and unaffected by the influx of tourists.

◄ San Giorgio Maggiore

# Ideas

## The big six

In effect all of central Venice is one colossal sight, and you'd have a great time if you were to spend your days here just wandering the alleyways at leisure. That said, there are several specific **monuments** and **museums** you really should make a point of visiting. Here are six of Venice's foremost attractions, every one of which is guaranteed to amaze.

### The Palazzo Ducale

The home of the doges was the nerve-centre of the entire Venetian empire, and was decorated by some of the greatest Venetian artists.

▶ P.54 ▶ SAN MARCO: THE PIAZZA  ▲

### The Frari

The gargantuan edifice of Santa Maria Gloriosa dei Frari contains masterpieces by Titian, Bellini, Donatello and many more.

▶ P.96 ▶ SAN POLO & SANTA CROCE  ▲

## San Marco

The mosaic-encrusted church of Saint Mark is the most opulent cathedral in all of Europe.

▶ P.52 ▶ SAN MARCO: THE PIAZZA ▼

## The Scuola Grande di San Rocco

Rome has the Sistine Chapel, Florence has the Brancacci Chapel, and Venice has the Scuola Grande di San Rocco, with its overwhelming cycle of paintings by Jacopo Tintoretto.

▶ P.98 ▶ SAN POLO & SANTA CROCE ▲

## The Accademia

In the Accademia's magnificent galleries you can trace the development of painting in Venice from the fifteenth century to the eighteenth, the last golden age of Venetian art.

▶ P.77 ▶
DORSODURO ▶

## Santi Giovanni e Paolo

The vast Dominican church of Santi Giovanni e Paolo is the mausoleum of the doges, containing some of the city's finest sculpture.

▶ P.116 ▶
CENTRAL CASTELLO ◀

## The main islands

The 118 islets of the historic centre could keep you fully occupied for weeks, but even on a short trip you should try to find time for an expedition to some of the **outlying islands** of the lagoon. Go to Torcello and you'll be standing on the spot where the history of Venice began; on Murano and Burano you'll get an insight into crafts that have been central to Venetian self-identity for centuries; and an hour on Giudecca will reveal evidence that the city is nowhere near as moribund as some people like to make out.

### Murano

Glass has been the basis of Murano's economy for seven hundred years, and there are still plenty of factories where you can admire the glassblowers' amazing skills.

▶ P.141 ▶ THE NORTHERN ISLANDS ▲

### Burano

The brightly painted exteriors of the houses of Burano give this island an appearance that's distinct from any other settlement in the lagoon.

▶ P.143 ▶ THE NORTHERN ISLANDS ▲

## San Michele

Located a short distance north of the city centre, San Michele is possibly the most beautiful cemetery in the world.

▸ P.140 ▸ **THE NORTHERN ISLANDS** ▸

## Torcello

The majestic cathedral of Torcello – the oldest building in the whole lagoon – marks the spot where the lagoon city came into existence.

▸ P.144 ▸ **THE NORTHERN ISLANDS** ▾

## La Giudecca

Once one of the city's main industrial zones, La Giudecca is nowadays a predominantly residential area that retains much of the spirit of the city prior to the age of mass tourism

▸ P.150 ▸ **THE SOUTHERN ISLANDS** ▾

## Venice viewpoints

Girdled with water, replete with beautiful buildings, flanked by the sea and overlooked by the snow-capped peaks of the Dolomites, Venice is the most photogenic of cities. Stand on any bridge and you'll have material for a dozen photographs staring you in the face. For great **panoramic views** of the place, however, you should make a bee-line for one or more of these vantage points.

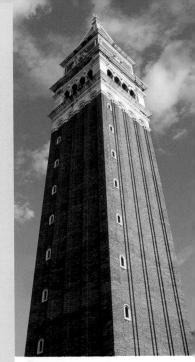

### Campanile di San Marco

The cathedral's belltower – the tallest structure for miles around – affords grand-stand views of the historic centre.

▸ P.57 ▸ SAN MARCO: THE PIAZZA

### The walk to Sant'Elena

A stroll from the Palazzo Ducale to Sant'Elena – the eastern limit of the city – gives you an unforgettable and ever-changing panorama.

▸ P.129 ▸ EASTERN CASTELLO

## San Giorgio Maggiore

The one thing you can't see from the Campanile di San Marco is the Campanile di San Marco, which is why the best of all views to be had is from the belltower of San Giorgio Maggiore, across the water.

▶ P.148 ▶ THE SOUTHERN ISLANDS ▶

## The boat to Burano

For a long-range perspective on the whole of the city, take a trip on the #LN boat from Fondamente Nove out to Burano.

▶ P.140 ▶ THE NORTHERN ISLANDS ◀

## The Záttere

The southern waterfront of Dorsoduro, formerly a busy dock, is nowadays a perfect place for an unhurried stroll and café-stop.

▶ P.81 ▶ DORSODURO ▶

## Byzantine Venice

The Venetian lagoon was first settled in the fifth century, by people fleeing from the hordes of Attila the Hun, and from its inception their confederation of tiny settlements owed allegiance to **Byzantium**. The cultural influence of the capital of the Eastern Roman Empire continued to be felt long after the Venetians achieved their political independence. Signs of this crucial relationship are evident all over the city, both in its **churches** and in its **palaces**.

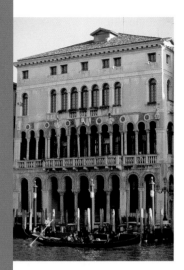

### Palazzo Loredan

The Palazzo Loredan was founded way back in the thirteenth century; as was the adjacent Palazzo Farsetti; together they now function as the town hall.

▶ **P.135** ▶ **THE CANAL GRANDE**　▲

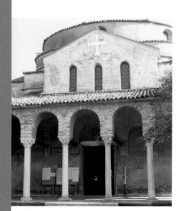

### Santa Fosca

Standing next to Torcello's cathedral, the plain little church of Santa Fosca clearly shows its Byzantine heritage.

▶ **P.145** ▶ **THE NORTHERN ISLANDS**　▲

## Museo Dipinti Sacri Bizantini

The city's Greek community kept alive the tradition of Byzantine icon painting for centuries, as you'll see in this museum.

▶ P.121 ▶ CENTRAL CASTELLO ▼

## San Giacomo di Rialto

Traditionally regarded as the oldest church in central Venice, San Giacomo di Rialto is Byzantine in design and adorned by columns of ancient Greek marble.

▶ P.91 ▶ SAN POLO & SANTA CROCE ▼

## Ca' da Mosto

Dating back to the thirteenth century, this picturesque Canal Grande palazzo is a superb example of the distinctive hybrid of Veneto-Byzantine architecture.

▶ P.134 ▶ THE CANAL GRANDE ▲

## The Pala d'Oro

The mosaics of San Marco owe much to the style of Byzantium, and Byzantine goldsmiths and jewellers were responsible for much of the handiwork on the astounding Pala d'Oro.

▶ P.54 ▶ SAN MARCO: THE PIAZZA ▲

## Museums and art galleries

The **Accademia** packs a bigger punch than any other of the city's **museums** and **galleries**, so if you have time for only one collection the choice is pretty straightforward. But it would be a shame not to sample the other offerings, which include comprehensive surveys of Venetian political, social and maritime history, a superb overview of eighteenth-century art, and an assembly of some of the key figures of modern art.

### The Guggenheim

For a break from the Renaissance, spend an hour or two with the Guggenheim's fine array of twentieth-century art.

▸ P.79 ▸ DORSODURO ▲

### Museo Storico Navale

As you'd expect from a city whose wealth and power was founded on shipping, the naval museum offers a comprehensive overview of maritime history and technology.

▸ P.128 ▸ EASTERN CASTELLO ▲

## Ca' d'Oro

Once the most extravagant house on the Canal Grande, the Ca' d'Oro today is home to an engagingly miscellaneous art collection.

▸ P.110 ▸
CANNAREGIO ▸

## Ca' Rezzonico

Devoted to the visual and applied arts of the eighteenth century, the Ca' Rezzonico contains several wonderful paintings and some frankly bizarre furniture.

▸ P.85 ▸
DORSODURO ▾

## Museo Correr

Now joined to the Libreria Sansoviniana and the archeological museum, the Correr is a museum of Venetian history with an excellent art gallery upstairs.

▸ P.59 ▸ SAN MARCO:
THE PIAZZA ▸

# Renaissance architecture

An enduring taste for colourful surface decoration and intricate stone-carving is in evidence in Venice right to the end of the fifteenth century, long after the rigorous classical precepts of **Renaissance architecture** had gained currency elsewhere in Italy. By the end of the following century, however, the more severe style of the Padua-born architect **Andrea Palladio** – whose buildings have become an intrinsic part of the image of Venice – had become the model for church design throughout Europe.

### Palazzo Grimani

It took nearly twenty years to build the Palazzo Grimani, the most intimidating palace on the Canal Grande.

▸ P.135 ▸ THE CANAL GRANDE ▲

### The Redentore

Overlooking the city from the centre of the Giudecca waterfront, the Redentore is the greatest of Palladio's Venetian churches.

▸ P.150 ▸ SOUTHERN ISLANDS ▼

## San Salvador

Outside it doesn't look terribly impressive, but the interior of San Salvador is an imposing example of Renaissance orderliness.

▶ P.64 ▶ SAN MARCO: NORTH OF THE PIAZZA ▲

## San Michele in Isola

Designed by Mauro Codussi, this beguiling little church was one of the first Renaissance buildings in Venice.

▶ P.140 ▶ THE NORTHERN ISLANDS ▼

## The Procuratie Vecchie

The former offices of the administrators of the Basilica di San Marco fill one whole side of the Piazza, contributing to a magnificent architectural set-piece.

▶ P.58 ▶ SAN MARCO: THE PIAZZA ▼

## The Libreria Sansoviniana and the Zecca

Standing side by side opposite the Palazzo Ducale, the city library and mint were both designed by Jacopo Sansovino, the Republic's principal architect in the early sixteenth century.

▶ P.61 ▶ SAN MARCO: THE PIAZZA ▲

## Eighteenth-century art

The **eighteenth century** was the period of Venice's terminal decline as a political and economic force – with the coming of Napoleon, the Republic was dead. Yet the visual arts underwent a remarkable resurgence at this time, with painters such as **Tiepolo** (father and son), **Canaletto** and the **Guardi** brothers at the forefront. First stop for a survey of eighteenth-century art is the Accademia, then the Ca' Rezzonico. After those, check out some of the following.

### Santa Maria della Fava

The two Giambattistas – Tiepolo and Piazzetta – can be seen together in the modest church of Santa Maria della Fava.

▸ P.119 ▸ CENTRAL CASTELLO ▲

### Palazzo Querini-Stampalia

The gallery's charmingly clumsy paintings by Gabriel Bella provide a fascinating chronicle of daily life in eighteenth-century Venice.

▸ P.119 ▸ CENTRAL CASTELLO ▲

## Angelo Raffaele

The organ loft of Angelo Raffaele is decorated with an enchanting sequence of pictures depicting scenes from the life of St Tobias.

▶ P.83 ▶ DORSODURO ▶

## The Gesuati

As well as a superb ceiling by Giambattista Tiepolo, the Gesuati has altarpieces by two other giants of eighteenth-century painting, Giambattista Piazzetta and Sebastiano Ricci.

▶ P.81 ▶ DORSODURO ▼

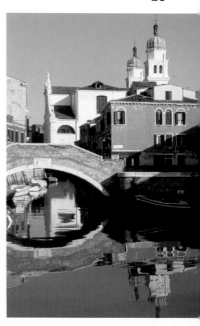

## Palazzo Labia

Giambattista Tiepolo was also the creator of some seductive secular paintings, a superb example being his work in the ballroom of the Palazzo Labia.

▶ P.106 ▶ CANNAREGIO ▶

## Shops and markets

Venice is a small city, with a population of less than 70,000 in the historic centre, so it should be no surprise to find that it doesn't have shopping streets to compare with those of Milan, Florence or Rome. But many of the big Italian fashion labels have outlets in the **Mercerie** and to the **west of the Piazza**, and there are several places where you can buy something uniquely Venetian – and the **Rialto** remains one of Europe's most characterful marketplaces.

### Lace

Like Murano in the northern lagoon, Burano has its own specialist handicraft – exquisite lacework.

▶ P.143 ▶ THE NORTHERN ISLANDS ▲

### Paper

Decorative paper is another Venetian speciality, sold through various small outlets, such as Legatoria Piazzesi.

▶ P.73 ▶ SAN MARCO: WEST OF THE PIAZZA ▲

## Glass

No trip to Venice would be complete without a visit to the furnaces and shops of Murano.

> P.141 ▶ THE NORTHERN ISLANDS ▼

## Masks

Carnival masks are made year-round in the city's numerous workshops, and their handiwork is amazingly inventive – MondoNovo is one of the very best.

> P.86 ▶ DORSODURO ▲

## The Rialto

Once the most celebrated market in Europe, the Rialto is nowadays a more humble but still thriving operation, offering a fabulous array of fresh food – plus thousands of souvenir T-shirts.

> P.89 ▶ SAN POLO & SANTA CROCE ◀

## The Mercerie

Running from the Piazza to within a few metres of the Rialto Bridge, the Mercerie are the busiest shopping streets in Venice.

> P.63 ▶ SAN MARCO: NORTH OF THE PIAZZA ▶

## Death in Venice

Often devastated by plague and always prey to a host of swamp-bound diseases, Venice was inextricably linked with the idea of death long before Thomas Mann welded the two words together. The **cemetery island** of San Michele and the **churches** of Santi Giovanni e Paolo and the Frari are essential sights for tomb connoisseurs, and elsewhere in the city there's plenty to interest the morbidly minded.

### The Lido

The beach and the grand hotels of the Lido provided the setting for Thomas Mann's great novella *Death in Venice* and Visconti's film of the book.

▶ P.151 ▶ THE SOUTHERN ISLANDS ▲

### Campo San Polo

Bullfights used to be a regular event on Campo San Polo, which also saw the murder of a member of Florence's mighty Medici clan.

▶ P.95 ▶ SAN POLO & SANTA CROCE ▲

## Palazzo Vendramin-Calergi

Richard Wagner died in the Palazzo Vendramin-Calergi in February 1883; the building is now home to Venice's casino.

▶ P.131 ▶ THE CANAL GRANDE ▶

## San Giobbe

The church devoted to the long-suffering Job is home to one of the city's weirdest tombs.

▶ P.107 ▶ CANNAREGIO ◀

## Campo Novo

The stage-like Campo Novo, close to Santo Stefano church, is the lid of a vast pit for plague victims.

▶ P.73 ▶ SAN MARCO: WEST OF THE PIAZZA ▼

## Renaissance painting

From **Jacopo Bellini** and his sons (**Giovanni** and **Gentile**), through **Giorgione** and **Carpaccio**, to the mighty triumvirate of **Titian**, **Paolo Veronese** and **Tintoretto**, Venice nurtured some of the titanic figures of Renaissance art. To see some of the best of that era's paintings you should first visit the Accademia and Correr museums, the Palazzo Ducale and the Frari, then the scuole of San Rocco and San Giorgio degli Schiavoni. You're still far from finished, though, because many of Venice's churches retain the paintings they commissioned centuries ago.

### San Sebastiano

The parish church of Paolo Veronese is a treasure-house of pictures by the artist, begun before he had turned thirty.

▶ P.82 ▶ DORSODURO

### Madonna dell'Orto

Jacopo Tintoretto worshipped here, is buried here, and provided the church with a trio of mighty pictures.

▶ P.109 ▶ CANNAREGIO

## Santa Maria Formosa

A powerful image of Saint Barbara – a masterpiece by Palma il Vecchio – enhances a chapel in the church of Santa Maria Formosa.

▸ P.118 ▸ CENTRAL CASTELLO ▸

## San Zaccaria

A large and lustrous altarpiece by Giovanni Bellini is the highlight inside this wonderful building.

▸ P.119 ▸ CENTRAL CASTELLO ▾

## San Giorgio Maggiore

Tintoretto left his mark on San Giorgio Maggiore too – the chancel contains a pair of famous paintings created specifically for the place where they still hang.

▸ P.149 ▸ THE SOUTHERN ISLANDS ▾

## On the water

A lot of people come to Venice thinking that the only way to get around is by boat, and are surprised to find that they spend most of their time – if not all of it – walking from place to place, map in hand. But water is the lifeblood of Venice, and to appreciate the city properly you need to spend some time on the **canals** – and to take a look at the **Arsenale**, the gargantuan dockyard that was the foundation of the Republic's maritime power.

### Gondolas

Once an everyday means of transport round the lagoon, gondolas remain the quintessential Venetian trademark.

▸ P.171 ▸ DORSODURO ▲

### Boat passes

The moment you arrive in Venice, buy one of the various travel passes that are on offer, for unlimited use of the waterbus network.

▸ P.169 ▸ ESSENTIALS ▲

## The Arsenale

The powerhouse of the Venetian economy and the basis of its naval supremacy, the Arsenale was in effect a city within the city. Today it's mostly disused, but still redolent of former glories.

▸ P.127 ▸ EASTERN CASTELLO ◂

## Traghetti

Can't afford a jaunt on a gondola? Never mind – hop across the Canal Grande in a stand-up traghetto gondola instead.

▸ P.170 ▸ ESSENTIALS ▸

## The Canal Grande

Get on board the #1 vaporetto for an unhurried survey of the aquatic high street of Venice.

▸ P.169 ▸ ESSENTIALS ▾

## Venetian oddities

Maze-like, car-free and dilapidatedly durable, Venice in its entirety is a very strange place, and no matter how many times you return to the city it will never lose its aura of extreme peculiarity. Some details of the townscape are stranger than others, though. Here are a few **offbeat features** that are bound to stick in the memory.

### The Scala del Bovolo

The spiralling Scala del Bovolo features on thousands of postcards, but few visitors to the city ever manage to find it.

▶ P.66 ▶ SAN MARCO: NORTH OF THE PIAZZA

### Venetian dialect signs

The Venetian habit of slurring words and dropping syllables can produce some baffling names, none more so than San Zandegolà, or San Giovanni Decollato – Saint John the Beheaded.

▶ P.94 ▶ SAN POLO & SANTA CROCE ▲

## The Ospedaletto

From the grotesque decoration of its facade you might never guess that the Ospedaletto is actually a church.

▸ P.118 ▸ CENTRAL CASTELLO ▼

## Santa Maria del Giglio

The church of Saint Mary of the Lily is a monument to the glory of the people who paid for it rather than to the glory of God.

▸ P.71 ▸ SAN MARCO: WEST OF THE PIAZZA ▼

## Leaning towers

In a city built on mud it's inevitable that some of the taller structures – such as the campanile of Santo Stefano – should lurch a few degrees off the perpendicular.

▸ P.72 ▸ SAN MARCO: WEST OF THE PIAZZA ▲

## Gesuiti

At first sight the walls of the Gesuiti seem to be hung with damask; look again, and you'll see they're made of something quite different.

▸ P.111 ▸ CANNAREGIO ▼

## Multicultural Venice

As a thrustingly mercantile city, situated on the edge of the Mediterranean at the crossroads of Europe and Asia, Venice was always a place where a multitude of cultures mingled and did business. Many outsiders put down roots here and grew into significant communities; others have left fascinating evidence of their temporary residence.

**Fondaco dei Turchi**

HQ of the city's Turkish traders, the Fondaco dei Turchi is now occupied by the natural history museum.

▶ P.94 ▶ SAN POLO & SANTA CROCE  ▲

**Scuola degli Albanesi**

Some lovely pieces of sculpture identify this tiny building as the former hub of Venice's Albanian community.

▶ P.72 ▶ SAN MARCO:
WEST OF THE PIAZZA  ▲

### San Lazzaro degli Armeni

The Armenian island of San Lazzaro offers one of the lagoon's most intriguing guided tours, given by the monastery's multilingual residents.

▸ P.153 ▸ **THE SOUTHERN ISLANDS** ▼

### San Giorgio dei Greci

A precariously tilting tower marks out the church that for centuries was the spiritual centre of Venice's sizeable Greek population.

▸ P.121 ▸ **CENTRAL CASTELLO** ▲

### The Fondaco dei Tedeschi

Once bustling with German merchants, the Fondaco dei Tedeschi is today the city's main post office.

▸ P.134 ▸ **THE CANAL GRANDE** ◀

### The Ghetto

The world's original ghetto is home to but a fraction of its former population, but it's still the centre of Jewish life in Venice.

▸ P.107 ▸ **CANNAREGIO** ▼

## Scuole

The religious confraternities known as **scuole** are distinctively Venetian institutions – dating back hundreds of years, some are still in existence today. All of them were formed to provide material and spiritual assistance to their members, but some were considerably wealthier than others, as you can see from the profusion of artworks that embellish the headquarters of the so-called Scuole Grande. The Scuola Grande di San Rocco is the most spectacular of them, but others repay a visit too.

### Scuola Grande dei Carmini

The scuola of the Carmelites is notable for yet another bravura ceiling by Giambattista Tiepolo.

▸ P.84 ▸ DORSODURO    ▲

### Scuola di Battioro e Tiraoro

Looking something like an overgrown cabinet, the tiny scuola of Venice's gold-smiths is tucked alongside the church of San Stae, right on the Canal Grande.

▸ P.93 ▸ SAN POLO & SANTA CROCE    ▲

### Scuola di San Giorgio degli Schiavoni

The Slavs' scuola features on many visitors' lists of favourite places in Venice, on account of Carpaccio's dazzling sequence of paintings in the lower hall.

▶ P.126 ▶ EASTERN CASTELLO ◀

### Scuola Grande di San Rocco

Still functioning today, the Scuola Grande di San Rocco is the wealthiest and most lavish of all the scuole.

▶ P.98 ▶ SAN POLO & SANTA CROCE ▼

### Scuola di San Giovanni Evangelista

The forecourt of the scuola of John the Baptist is one of the most alluring episodes in the Venetian cityscape.

▶ P.99 ▶ SAN POLO & SANTA CROCE ▶

### Scuola Grande di San Marco

Now Venice's hospital, the Scuola Grande di San Marco is a masterpiece of the early Renaissance, featuring carvings by Tullio and Antonio Lombardo, two of the major figures of the period.

▶ P.118 ▶ CENTRAL CASTELLO ◀

**Authentic Venice**

Around fifteen million people come here each year, and on a summer's day the influx of tourists exceeds the city's population. Most of these incomers see nothing but the Piazza, and if you never stray far from the precincts of the Basilica di San Marco it can seem that Venice has lost much of its soul to the depredations of modern tourism. Wander just a little further afield, however, and you'll find plentiful signs of the survival of a more authentic Venice.

### San Niccolò dei Mendicoli

Meander down to the western edge of Dorsoduro and you'll come to this quiet and ancient church, one of the most characterful in Venice.

▶ P.83 ▶ DORSODURO

### Campo Santa Maria Mater Domini

With its parish church, crumbling old houses, workadays bars and artisan's workshop, Campo Santa Maria Mater Domini is like a snapshot of an earlier age.

▶ P.92 ▶ SAN POLO & SANTA CROCE

## San Pietro di Castello

Marooned on the edge of the city, the former cathedral presides over a district where boat-maintenance is the main business.

▸ P.128 ▸ EASTERN CASTELLO ▾

## Campo San Giacomo dell'Orio

The area around the church of San Giacomo dell'Orio is spacious and underpopulated, as it lies off the beaten track for the majority of visitors.

▸ P.94 ▸ SAN POLO & SANTA CROCE ▴

## Northern Cannaregio

On any day of the year, residents far outnumber tourists on the long canalside pavements of northern Cannaregio.

▸ P.108 ▸ CANNAREGIO ▾

**Food and drink**

More than anywhere else in Italy, the division between bars and restaurants is often difficult to draw in Venice. Almost every bar serves sandwiches at least, while a distinctive aspect of the Venetian social scene is the **bacarò**, which is essentially a bar that serves a range of snacks called **cicheti**, plus sometimes more substantial meals. Conversely, many restaurants are fronted by a **bar**, which may stay open long after the kitchen has shut down for the night.

### Wine bars

The Veneto produces more DOC (Denominazione di origine controllata) wine than any other region of Italy, so it's no surprise that it's bursting with bars in which you can sample Valpolicella, Bardolino, Soave and Prosecco, the last a light, champagne-like wine from the area around Conegliano. Al Volto has the city's widest selection.

▸ P.68 ▸ SAN MARCO: NORTH OF THE PIAZZA ▲

### Seafood

Venice has dozens of restaurants, some very good, some very bad, some very expensive, many not, but almost all of them have one thing in common: seafood dominates the menu. Visit the Rialto fish market for an overview of what's on offer.

▸ P.90 ▸ SAN POLO & SANTA CROCE ▲

## Cafés

Europe's first café opened in Venice in 1683, and within a few decades Goldoni had created a play in which the hero, a café owner, declared "my profession is necessary to the glory of the city". Coffee culture is still crucial to Venetian life, with every parish having its busy café-cum-social-centre.

▶ P.62 ▶ SAN MARCO: THE PIAZZA ▶

## Gelati

Every Italian city has its makers of sinful homemade ice cream, and Venice has some of the best. Don't go home without sampling the products of Paolin, or Nico, or Causin.

▶ P.74 ▶ SAN MARCO:
WEST OF THE PIAZZA ◀

## Cicheti and sandwiches

Virtually all bars will have a selection of plump *tramezzini* (sandwiches) at lunchtime, and in many – such as the Osteria alle Botteghe – you'll find an enticing array of *cicheti*, typically including *polpette* (small beef and garlic meatballs), *carciofini* (artichoke hearts) and *polipi* (baby octopus or squid).

▶ P.75 ▶ SAN MARCO:
WEST OF THE PIAZZA ▼

## Pasticcerie

Venetian pastries are as delicious as any in Italy. Look out for the Antichi Pasticceri Venexiani sign: membership of this group signifies high standards and top-quality ingredients. No standards – or prices – are higher than those at the famous Marchini.

▶ P.67 ▶ SAN MARCO:
NORTH OF THE PIAZZA ▲

## Music in Venice

The music written and performed in San Marco was imitated by composers all over Europe, and for a long time Venice was the world's greatest centre for **opera** – around five hundred works received their first performances here in the first half of the eighteenth century. And Venice was home to the composer of the **Four Seasons**, the most frequently recorded of all classical pieces. As you might expect in a city with a dearth of native teenagers, the **live music** scene isn't too exciting, but the university population ensures the presence of a few lively bars, some of which double up as live music venues.

### Monteverdi

The greatest of all Venetian composers wrote sacred music for San Marco and operas for the San Cassian opera house, and is buried in the Frari.

▶ P.97 ▶ SAN POLO & SANTA CROCE ▲

### Palazzo Pisani

Venice's conservatory of music is now housed in the vast Palazzo Pisani, the ostentatious home of the grotesquely wealthy Pisani family.

▶ P.73 ▶ SAN MARCO:
WEST OF THE PIAZZA ▲

## Palazzi Giustinian

The double palace of the Palazzi Giustinian was for a while the home of Richard Wagner, who wrote part of *Tristan und Isolde* here.

▶ P.138 ▶ THE CANAL GRANDE ▶

## Paradiso Perduto

Nightlife in Venice is pretty tame, but the buzzing Paradiso Perduto – one of Venice's liveliest bars – often has live music and DJs.

▶ P.113 ▶ CANNAREGIO ▼

## The Pietà

Vivaldi wrote some of his finest music for the orphanage of the Pietà, where he was violin-master and choirmaster.

▶ P.121 ▶ CENTRAL CASTELLO ▼

## Teatro Malibran

Closed for decades, the historic Malibran is now restored and back in business as the city's main concert hall.

▶ P.123 ▶ CENTRAL CASTELLO ◀

## Crime and punishment

It may not have produced monsters to compare with the Borgias and the other murderous clans of Renaissance Italy, but Venice's reputation was far from spotless: the **Council of Ten** (in effect the department of state security) was once regarded with the same sort of dread as Stalin's secret police, and the city's **prisons** were notorious far beyond the city's boundaries. Various sites around the city have dark associations.

### The Piazzetta columns

Many a felon's life came to an end on the executioner's block between the twin columns of the Piazzetta, a place whose grisly aura lives on in Venetian superstition.

▸ P.60 ▸ SAN MARCO: THE PIAZZA ▲

### The Gobbo di Rialto

Misbehaving Venetians were sometimes told to report to the Gobbo di Rialto for a particularly embarrassing form of punishment.

▸ P.92 ▸ SAN POLO & SANTA CROCE ▲

## Paolo Sarpi

Brilliant scientist and dauntless defender of Venice's independence from papal interference, Father Sarpi fell foul of the Vatican and was targetted by its hired assassins.

▶ P.110 ▶ CANNAREGIO ▼

## Campo San Zaccaria

In the ninth century a doge was murdered outside the church of San Zaccaria; three hundred years later another doge suffered the same fate.

▶ P.120 ▶ CENTRAL CASTELLO ▼

## The Bridge of Sighs

Towards the end of your visit to the Palazzo Ducale, you cross the bridge by which prisoners were led to their cells on the other side of the canal.

▶ P.57 ▶ SAN MARCO: THE PIAZZA ▲

## La Fenice

People went to prison for burning down the opera house in 1996, but many are sceptical that the real villains have been caught.

▶ P.70 ▶ SAN MARCO:
WEST OF THE PIAZZA ▲

**Festivals**

Venice celebrates enthusiastically a number of **special days** either not observed elsewhere in Italy, or, like the Carnevale, celebrated to a lesser extent. Although they have gone through various degrees of decline and revival, the form they take now is still related very strongly to their traditional character. In addition to these, Venice can boast two of the continent's most prestigious **cultural events**: the annual film festival and the Biennale art show, which – as the name says – takes place in alternate years.

### The Regata Storica

A flotilla of ornate antique boats makes its way down the Canal Grande to mark the start of the Regata Storica, the year's big event for Venice's gondoliers.

▶ P.173 ▶ ESSENTIALS

### The Film Festival

Glamour and controversy always share top billing at Venice's annual film festival.

▶ P.172 ▶ ESSENTIALS

## La Vogalonga

The "long row" is the most arduous of Venice's numerous rowing races, inflicting 32 kilometres of suffering on the competing crews.

▸ P.173 ▸ ESSENTIALS ▲

## Carnevale

Italy's wildest fancy-dress party fills the ten days leading to Shrove Tuesday and draws revellers from all over the world.

▸ P.173 ▸ ESSENTIALS ▲

## The Biennale

It's been going for more than a hundred years, and the Biennale remains the art world's most prestigious jamboree.

▸ P.172 ▸ ESSENTIALS ▲

## Festa del Redentore

Celebrating the city's deliverance from plague, the Redentore festival culminates with spectacular volleys of fireworks.

▸ P.173 ▸ ESSENTIALS ▲

## Festa della Salute

The Salute church is the focal point of another festival giving thanks for the restoration of the city's health (*salute*) after a terrible pestilence.

▸ P.173 ▸ ESSENTIALS ◀

# Places

# Places

# San Marco: the Piazza

The sestiere of San Marco – a rectangle smaller than 1000m by 500m – has been the nucleus of Venice from the start of the city's existence. When its founders decamped from the coastal town of Malamocco to settle on the safer islands of the inner lagoon, the area now known as the **Piazza San Marco** was where the first rulers built their citadel – the **Palazzo Ducale** – and it was here that they established their most important church – the **Basilica di San Marco**. Over the succeeding centuries the Basilica evolved into the most ostentatiously rich church in Christendom, and the Palazzo Ducale grew to accommodate and celebrate a system of government that endured for longer than any other republican regime in Europe. Meanwhile, the setting for these two great edifices developed into a public space so dignified that no other square in the city was thought fit to bear the name "piazza" – all other Venetian squares are campi or campielli.

Nowadays the Piazza is what keeps the city solvent: the plushest hotels are concentrated in the San Marco sestiere; the most elegant and exorbitant cafés spill out onto the pavement from the Piazza's arcades; the most

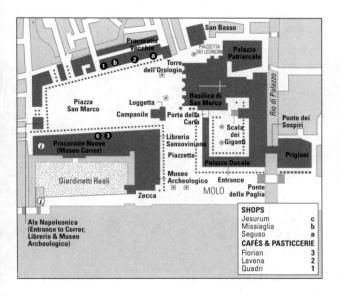

extravagantly priced seafood is served in this area's restaurants; and the swankiest shops in Venice line the Piazza and the streets radiating from it.

## The Basilica di San Marco

Open to tourists Mon–Sat 9.30am–5.30pm, Sun 2–4pm, though the Loggia dei Cavalli is open Sun morning. All over Venice you see images of the lion of St Mark holding a book on which is carved the text "Pax tibi, Marce evangelista meus. Hic requiescet corpus tuum" ("Peace be with you Mark, my Evangelist. Here shall your body rest"). These supposedly are the words with which St Mark was greeted by an angel who appeared to him on the night he took shelter in the lagoon on his way back to Rome. Having thus assured themselves of the sacred ordination of their city, the first Venetians duly went about fulfilling the angelic prophecy. In 828 two merchants stole the body of St Mark from its tomb in Alexandria and brought it back to Venice. Work began immediately on a shrine to

house him, and the Basilica di San Marco was consecrated in 832. The amazing church you see today is essentially the version built in 1063–94, embellished in the succeeding centuries.

The marble-clad **exterior** is adorned with numerous pieces of ancient stonework, but a couple of features warrant special attention: the Romanesque carvings of the arches of the central doorway; and the group of porphyry figures set into the wall on the waterfront side – known as the Tetrarchs, in all likelihood a fourth-century Egyptian work depicting Diocletian and the three colleagues with whom he ruled the unravelling Roman Empire. The real **horses of San Marco** are inside the church – the four outside are modern replicas. On the main facade, the only ancient mosaic to survive is *The Arrival of the Body of St Mark*, above the

▼ EXTERIOR OF BASILICA

▲ THE HORSES OF SAN MARCO

Porta di Sant'Alipio (far left); made around 1260, it features the earliest known image of the Basilica.

Just inside, the intricately patterned stonework of the narthex floor is mostly eleventh- and twelfth-century, while the majority of the mosaics on the domes and arches constitute a series of Old Testament scenes dating from the thirteenth century. Three doges (see p.55) and one dogaressa have tombs in the narthex. That of Vitale Falier, the doge who consecrated the Basilica in 1094, is the oldest funerary monument in Venice – it's at the base of the first arch.

On the right of the main door from the narthex into the body of the church is a steep staircase up to the **Museo Marciano** and the **Loggia dei Cavalli** (daily: summer 9.45am–5pm; winter 9.30am–4pm; €1.50), home of the fabled horses. Thieved from Constantinople in 1204, the horses are almost certainly Roman works of the second century, and are the only *quadriga* (group of four horses harnessed to a chariot) to have survived from the Classical world.

With its undulating floor of patterned marble, its plates of eastern stone on the lower walls, and its 4000 square metres of mosaic covering every other inch of wall and vaulting, the golden **interior** of San Marco achieves a hypnotic effect. There's too much to take in at one go: the only way to do it justice is to call in for at least half an hour at the beginning and end of a couple of days. Simply to list the highlights would take pages, but be sure to make time for a good look at the following **mosaics**, nearly all of which date from the twelfth and thirteenth centuries: the west dome, showing *Pentecost*; the *Betrayal of Christ*, *Crucifixion*, *Marys at the Tomb*, *Descent into Limbo* and *Incredulity of Thomas*, on the arch between west and central domes; the central dome, depicting the *Ascension*, *Virgin with Angels and Apostles*, *Virtues and Beatitudes*, *Evangelists*, *Four Allegories of the Holy Rivers*; the east dome, illustrating *The Religion of Christ Foretold by the Prophets*; the *Four Patron Saints of Venice*, between the windows of the apse (created around 1100 and thus among the earliest works in San Marco); and the

▲ THE MOSAICS

huge *Agony in the Garden* on the wall of the south aisle.

Officially the remains of Saint Mark lie in the sarcophagus underneath the high altar, at the back of which you can see the most precious of San Marco's treasures, the astonishing **Pala d'Oro** (summer Mon–Sat 9.45am–5pm, Sun 2–5pm; winter closes 4pm; €1.50) – the "golden altar screen". Commissioned in 976 in Constantinople, the *Pala* was enlarged, enriched and rearranged by Byzantine goldsmiths in 1105, then by Venetians in 1209 to incorporate some of the less cumbersome loot from the Fourth Crusade, and again (finally) in 1345.

Tucked into the corner of the south transept is the door of the **treasury** (summer Mon–Sat 9.45am–5pm, Sun 2–5pm; winter closes 4pm; €2). This dazzling warehouse of chalices, icons, reliquaries, candelabra and other ecclesiastical appurtenances is an unsurpassed collection of Byzantine silver and gold work.

Back in the main body of the Basilica, don't overlook the pavement – laid out in the twelfth and thirteenth centuries, it's an intriguing patchwork of abstract shapes and religious symbols. Another marvel is the rood screen, surmounted by marble figures of The Virgin, St Mark and the Apostles (1394) by Jacobello and Pietro Paolo Dalle Masegne. Finally, Venice's most revered religious image, the tenth-century **Icon of the Madonna of Nicopeia**, stands in the chapel on the east side of the north transept; until 1204 it was one of the most revered icons in Constantinople, where it used to be carried ceremonially at the head of the emperor's army.

### The Palazzo Ducale

Daily: April–Oct 9am–7pm, last tickets 5.30pm; Nov–March 9am–5pm, last tickets 3.30pm. Entrance with the Museum Card – see p.171.
Architecturally, the Palazzo Ducale is a unique mixture: the style of its exterior, with its geometrically patterned stonework and continuous tracery walls, can only be called Islamicized Gothic, whereas the courtyards and much of the interior are based on Classical forms – a blending of influences that led Ruskin to declare it "the central building of the world". Unquestionably, it is the finest secular building of its era in Europe, and the central building

## The government of Venice

Virtually from the beginning, the **government of Venice** was dominated by the merchant class, who in 1297 enacted a measure known as the **Serrata del Maggior Consiglio** (Closure of the Great Council). From then onwards, any man not belonging to one of the wealthy families on the list compiled for the *Serrata* was ineligible to participate in the running of the city. After a while, this list was succeeded by a register of patrician births and marriages called the **Libro d'Oro**, upon which all claims to membership of the elite were based. By the second decade of the fourteenth century, the constitution of Venice had reached a form that was to endure until the coming of Napoleon; its civil and criminal code, defined in the early thirteenth century, was equally resistant to change.

What made the political system stable was its web of counterbalancing councils and committees, and its exclusion of any youngsters. Most patricians entered the Maggior Consiglio at 25 and could not expect a middle-ranking post before 45; from the middle ranks to the top was another long haul – the average age of the **doge** from 1400 to 1600 was 72. The doge was **elected for life** and sat on all the major councils of state, which made him extremely influential in the formation of policy. The dogeship was the monopoly of old men not solely because of the celebrated Venetian respect for the wisdom of the aged, but also because a man in his seventies would have fewer opportunities to abuse the unrivalled powers of the dogeship.

of Venice: it was the residence of the doge, the home of all of Venice's governing councils, its law courts, a sizeable number of its civil servants and even its prisons. All power in the Venetian Republic and its domains was controlled within this building.

The original doge's fortress was founded at the start of the ninth century, but it was in the fourteenth and fifteenth centuries that the Palazzo Ducale acquired its present shape. The principal entrance, the Porta della Carta, was commissioned in 1438 by Doge Francesco Fóscari, and is one of the most ornate Gothic works in the city. The passageway into the Palazzo ends under the Arco Fóscari, which you can see only after getting your ticket, as tourists are nowadays directed in through the arcades on the lagoon side.

From the ticket office you're directed straight into the **Museo dell'Opera**, where the originals of most of the superb capitals from the external loggias are well displayed. On the far side of the courtyard,

▼ SCALA DEI GIGANTI

opposite the entrance, stands the Arco Fóscari, facing the enormous staircase called the Scala dei Giganti. From ground level the traffic is directed up the Scala dei Censori to the upper arcade and thence up the gilded Scala d'Oro, the main internal staircase of the Palazzo Ducale. A subsidiary staircase on the right leads to the Doge's Apartments (look out for Titian's small fresco of *St Christopher*), then the Scala d'Oro continues up to the *secondo piano nobile* (see p.137), where you soon enter the **Anticollegio**. With its pictures by Tintoretto and Veronese, this is one of the richest rooms in the Palazzo Ducale, and no doubt made a suitable impact on the emissaries who waited here for admission to the Sala del Collegio, where the doge and his inner cabinet met. Ruskin maintained that in no other part of the palace could you "enter so deeply into the heart of Venice", though he was referring not to the mechanics of Venetian power but to the luscious cycle of ceiling paintings by Veronese.

Next door – the Sala del Senato – was where most major policies were determined. A motley collection of late

sixteenth-century artists produced the mechanically bombastic decoration of the walls and ceiling. Paolo Veronese again appears in the Sala del Consiglio dei Dieci, the room in which the much-feared Council of Ten discussed matters relating to state security. The unfortunates who were summoned before the Ten had to await their grilling in the next room, the Sala della Bussola; in the wall is a *Bocca di Leone* (Lion's Mouth), one of the boxes into which citizens could drop denunciations for the attention of the Ten and other state bodies.

Beyond the armoury, the Scala dei Censori takes you back to the second floor and the **Sala del Maggior Consiglio**, the assembly hall of all the Venetian patricians eligible to participate in the running of the city. This stupendous room, with its lavishly ornate ceiling, is dominated by the immense *Paradiso*, begun at the age of 77 by Tintoretto and completed by his son Domenico. Tintoretto was also commissioned to replace the room's frieze of portraits of the first 76 doges (the series continues in the Sala dello Scrutinio), but in the event Domenico and his

▼THE SALA DEL MAGGIOR CONSIGLIO

▲ THE PRISONS

assistants did the work. On the Piazzetta side the sequence is interrupted by a black veil, marking the place where Marin Falier would have been honoured had he not conspired against the state in 1355 and (as the lettering on the veil says) been beheaded for his crime.

A couple of rooms later, the route descends to the Magistrato alle Leggi, in which three works by Hieronymus Bosch are displayed: they were left to the Palazzo Ducale in the will of Cardinal Domenico Grimani, whose collection also provided the foundations of the city's archeological museum. The Scala dei Censori leads from here to the **Ponte dei Sospiri** (Bridge of Sighs) and the **Prigioni** (Prisons). Built in 1600, the bridge takes its popular name from the sighs of the prisoners who shuffled through its corridor. In reality, though, anyone passing this way had been let off pretty lightly. Hard cases were kept either in the sweltering Piombi (the Leads), under the roof of the Palazzo Ducale, or in the sodden gloom of the Pozzi (the Wells) in the bottom two storeys.

If you want to see the Piombi, and the rooms in which the day-to-day administration of Venice took place, take the Itinerari Segreti del Palazzo Ducale, a fascinating ninety-minute guided tour through the warren of offices and passageways that interlocks with the building's public rooms. (Tours in English daily at 9.55am, 10.45am & 11.35am; €12.50, €7 with Venice Card, includes entry to rest of palace. Tickets can be booked a minimum of two days in advance on ☎041.520.9070; for the next or same day go in person to Palazzo Ducale ticket desk to check availability.)

## The Campanile

Daily: April to mid-June 9am–7pm; mid-June to mid-Sept 9am–9pm; mid-Sept to March 9am–4pm. €6. The Campanile began life as a combined lighthouse and belltower, and was continually modified up to 1515, the year in which the golden angel was installed on the summit. Each of its five bells had a distinct

▼ THE CAMPANILE

function: the *Marangona*, the largest, tolled the beginning and end of the working day; the *Trottiera* was a signal for members of the Maggior Consiglio to hurry along; the *Nona* rang midday; the *Mezza Terza* announced a session of the Senate; and the smallest, the *Renghiera* or *Maleficio*, gave notice of an execution. But the Campanile's most dramatic contribution to the history of the city was made on July 14, 1902, the day on which, at 9.52am, it fell down. The town councillors decided that evening that the Campanile should be rebuilt "dov'era e com'era" (where it was and how it was), and a decade later, on St Mark's Day 1912, the new tower was opened, in all but minor details a replica of the original. At 99m, the Campanile is the tallest structure in the city, and from the top you can make out virtually every building, but not a single canal.

### The Torre dell'Orologio

The other tower in the Piazza, the Torre dell'Orologio (Clock Tower), was built between 1496 and 1506. Legend relates that the makers of the clock slaved away for three years at their project, only to have their eyes put out so that they couldn't repeat their engineering marvel for other patrons. In fact the pair received a generous pension – presumably too dull an outcome for the city's folklorists. The tower's roof terrace supports two bronze wild men known as "The Moors", because of their dark patina. A protracted restoration of the Torre dell'Orologio is drawing to a close; when it's over, it will be possible to climb

▲ THE TORRE DELL'OROLOGIO

up through the innards of the tower, to the terrace from which the Moors strike the hour.

### The Procuratie

Away to the left of the Torre dell'Orologio stretches the **Procuratie Vecchie**, begun around 1500, to designs by Mauro Codussi, who also designed much of the clock tower. Once the home of the Procurators of San Marco, whose responsibilities included the upkeep of the Basilica and the administration of the other government-owned properties, the block earned substantial rents for the city coffers: the upper floors housed some of the choicest apartments in town, while the ground floor was leased to shopkeepers and craftsmen, as is still the case.

Within a century or so, the procurators were moved across the Piazza to new premises, the **Procuratie Nuove**. When Napoleon's stepson, Eugène Beauharnais, was the Viceroy of Italy, he appropriated this building as a royal palace, and then discovered that the accommodation lacked a ballroom. He duly demolished the church of San Geminiano, which had filled part of the third side of the Piazza, and connected the Procuratie Nuove and Vecchie with a new wing, the **Ala Napoleonica**, containing the essential facility.

### The Correr and archeological museums

Daily: April–Oct 9am–7pm; Nov–March 9am–5pm; last tickets 90min before closing. Entrance with Museum Card – see p.171. Many of the rooms in the Ala Napoleonica and Procu-ratie Nuove are now occupied by the **Museo Correr**, the civic museum of Venice, which is joined to the archeological museum and Sansovino's superb library, the Libreria Sansoviniana (see p.61).

Nobody could make out that the immense Correr collection is consistently fascinating, but it incorporates a picture gallery that more than makes up for the duller stretches, and its sections on Venetian society contain some eye-opening exhibits. The first floor starts off with a gallery of Homeric reliefs by Canova, whose large self-portrait faces you as you enter; succeeding rooms display his *Daedalus and Icarus* (the group that made his name at the age of 21), his faux-modest *Venus Italica* and some of the rough clay models he created as first drafts for his classically poised sculptures. After that you're into

the historical collection, which will be intermittently enlightening if your Italian is good and you already have a pretty wide knowledge of Venetian history. Then you pass through an armoury and an exhibition of small bronze sculptures before entering the **Museo Archeologico**. It's a somewhat scrappy and uninspiring museum, but look out for a head of Athena from the fourth century BC, a trio of wounded Gallic warriors (Roman copies of Hellenistic originals) and a phalanx of Roman emperors.

At the furthest point of the archeological museum a door opens into the hall of Sansovino's library. Back in the Correr, a staircase beyond the sculpture section leads to the **Quadreria**, which may be no rival for the Accademia's collection but nonetheless sets out clearly the evolution of painting in Venice from the thirteenth century to around 1500, and does contain some gems, including Jacopo

▾ ENTRANCE TO THE CORRER

de'Barbari's astonishing aerial view of Venice, some remarkable pieces by Cosmè Tura and Antonello da Messina, and a roomful of work by the Bellini family. The Correr's best-known possession, however, is the **Carpaccio** painting of two terminally bored women once known as *The Courtesans*, though in fact it depicts a couple of late fifteenth-century bourgeois ladies dressed in a style at which none of their contemporaries would have raised an eyebrow. Carpaccio was once thought to be the painter of the *Portrait of a Young Man in a Red Hat*, another much-reproduced image, but it's now given to an anonymous painter from Ferrara or Bologna. The Correr also has a room of pictures from Venice's community of Greek artists, an immensely conservative group that nurtured the painter who later became known as El Greco – there's a picture by him here which you'd walk straight past if it weren't for the label.

From the Quadreria you're directed to the **Museo del Risorgimento**, which resumes the history of the city with its fall to Napoleon, then the itinerary passes through sections on Venetian festivals, crafts, trades and everyday life. Here the frivolous items are what catch the eye, especially a pair of eighteen-inch stacked shoes (as worn by the women in the Carpaccio painting), and an eighteenth-century portable hair-care kit that's the size of a suitcase. Finally you're steered down a corridor to the ballroom – a showcase for Canova's *Orpheus and Eurydice*, created in 1777, when the sculptor was still in his teens.

## The Piazzetta

For much of the Republic's existence, the Piazzetta – the open space between the Basilica and the waterfront – was the area where the councillors of Venice would gather to scheme and curry favour. The Piazzetta was also used for public executions: the usual site was the pavement between the two granite columns on the Molo, as this stretch of the waterfront is called.

▾ THE PIAZZETTA, WITH THE FACADE OF THE BIBLIOTECA

The last person to be executed here was one Domenico Storti, condemned to death in 1752 for the murder of his brother.

One of the columns is topped by a modern copy of a statue of St Theodore, the patron saint of Venice when it was dependent on Byzantium; the original, now on show in a corner of one of the Palazzo Ducale's courtyards, was a compilation of a Roman torso, a head of Mithridates the Great, and miscellaneous bits and pieces carved in Venice in the fourteenth century (the dragon included). The winged lion on the other column is an ancient 3000-kilo bronze beast that was converted into a lion of St Mark by jamming a Bible under its paws.

### The Libreria Sansoviniana

The Piazzetta is flanked by the Libreria Sansoviniana (or Biblioteca Marciana). The impetus to build the library came from the bequest of Cardinal Bessarion, who left his celebrated hoard of classical texts to the Republic in 1468. Bessarion's books and manuscripts were first housed in San Marco and then in the Palazzo Ducale, but finally it was decided that a special building was needed. Jacopo Sansovino got the job, but the library wasn't finished until 1591, two decades after his death. Contemporaries regarded the Libreria as one of the supreme designs of the era, and the main hall is certainly one of the most beautiful rooms in the city: paintings by Veronese, Tintoretto, Andrea Schiavone and others cover the walls and ceiling.

### The Zecca

Attached to the Libreria, with its main facade to the lagoon, is Sansovino's first major building in Venice, the Zecca or Mint. Constructed in stone and iron to make it fireproof (most stonework in Venice is just skin-deep), it was built between 1537 and 1545 on the site occupied by the mint since the thirteenth century. The rooms of the Mint are now part of the library, but are not open to tourists.

### The Giardinetti Reali

Beyond the Zecca, and behind a barricade of postcard and toy-gondola sellers, is a small public garden – the Giardinetti Reali – created by Eugène Beauharnais on the site of the state granaries. It's the nearest place to the centre where you'll find a bench and the shade of a tree, but in summer it's about as peaceful as a school playground. The spruced-up building at the foot of the nearby bridge is the Casino da Caffè, another legacy of the Napoleonic era, now the city's main tourist office.

# Shops

### Jesurum

Piazza San Marco 60–61. The finest Venetian lace, at prices that'll make you blink.

### Missiaglia

Piazza San Marco 125. Peerless and highly expensive gold and silver work from a jewellery firm that has a good claim to be Venice's classiest.

### Seguso

Piazza San Marco 143, @www.seguso.it. Traditional-style Murano glass, much of it created by the firm's founder, Archimede Seguso.

# Cafés and pasticcerie

### Florian

Piazza San Marco 56–59. Closed Wed in winter. Opened in 1720 by Florian Francesconi, and frescoed and mirrored in a passable pastiche of that period, this has long been the café to be seen in. A simple cappuccino will set you back around €8; if the resident musicians are playing, you'll be taxed another €4.50.

### Lavena

Piazza San Marco 133–134. Closed Tues in winter. Wagner's favourite café (there's a commemorative plaque inside) is the second member of the Piazza's top-bracket trio. For privacy you can take a table in the narrow little gallery overlooking the bar.

### Quadri

Piazza San Marco 120–124. Closed Mon in winter. In the same price league as *Florian*, but not quite as pretty. Austrian officers patronized it during the occupation, while the natives stuck with *Florian*, and it still has something of the air of being a runner-up in the society stakes.

▾ LAVENA

# San Marco: North of the Piazza

From the Piazza the bulk of the pedestrian traffic flows north to the **Rialto bridge** along the **Mercerie**, the most aggressive shopping mall in Venice. Only the churches of **San Giuliano** and **San Salvador** provide a diversion from the shops until you come to the **Campo San Bartolomeo**, the forecourt of the Rialto bridge and the locals' favoured spot for an after-work chat. Another square that's lively at the end of the day is the **Campo San Luca**, within a minute's stroll of *Al Volto*, the best-stocked *enoteca* in town. Secreted in the folds of the alleyways hereabouts is the spiralling staircase called the **Scala del Bovolo**. And slotted away in a tiny square close to the Canal Grande you'll find the most delicate of Venice's museum buildings – the Palazzo Pésaro degli Orfei, home of the **Museo Fortuny**.

## The Mercerie and San Giuliano

The **Mercerie**, a chain of streets that starts under the Torre dell'Orologio and finishes at the Campo San Bartolomeo, is the most direct route between San Marco and the Rialto and has always been a prime site for Venice's shopkeepers – its mixture of slickness and tackiness ensnares more shoppers than any other part of Venice. (Each of the five links in the chain is a *merceria*: Merceria dell'Orologio, di San Zulian, del Capitello, di San Salvador and 2 Aprile.)  Keep your eye open for one quirky feature: over the Sottoportego del Cappello (first left after the Torre) is a relief known as La Vecia del Morter – the Old Woman of the Mortar. The event it commemorates happened on the night of June 15, 1310, when the occupant of this house, an old woman named Giustina Rossi, looked out of her window and saw a contingent of Bajamonte Tiepolo's rebel army passing

▼ FACADE OF SAN GIULIANO

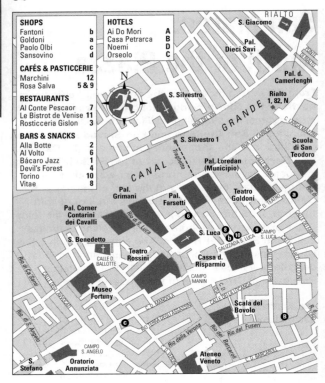

Map legend:

**SHOPS**
| | |
|---|---|
| Fantoni | b |
| Goldoni | a |
| Paolo Olbi | c |
| Sansovino | d |

**CAFÉS & PASTICCERIE**
| | |
|---|---|
| Marchini | 12 |
| Rosa Salva | 5 & 9 |

**RESTAURANTS**
| | |
|---|---|
| Al Conte Pescaor | 7 |
| Le Bistrot de Venise | 11 |
| Rosticceria Gislon | 3 |

**BARS & SNACKS**
| | |
|---|---|
| Alla Botte | 2 |
| Al Volto | 6 |
| Bácaro Jazz | 1 |
| Devil's Forest | 4 |
| Torino | 10 |
| Vitae | 8 |

**HOTELS**
| | |
|---|---|
| Ai Do Mori | A |
| Casa Petrarca | B |
| Noemi | D |
| Orseolo | C |

below. Possibly by accident, she knocked a stone mortar from her sill, and the missile landed on the skull of the standard-bearer, killing him outright. Seeing their flag go down, Tiepolo's troops panicked and fled.

Further on is the church of **San Giuliano** or San Zulian (Mon, Wed, Thurs & Sat 8.30am–noon & 3–6pm, Tues & Fri 8.30am–noon), rebuilt in the mid-sixteenth century with the generous aid of the physician Tommaso Rangone. His munificence and intellectual brilliance (but not his Christian faith) are attested by the Greek and Hebrew inscriptions on the facade and by Alessandro Vittoria's portrait statue above the door.

### San Salvador

Mon–Sat 9am–noon & 3–6pm, Sun 4–6pm. At its far end, the Mercerie veers right at the church of San Salvador or Salvatore, which was consecrated in 1177 by Pope Alexander III. The facade is less interesting than the interior, where, on the right-hand wall, you'll find Titian's *Annunciation* (1566), signed *"Fecit, fecit"* (Painted it, painted it), supposedly to emphasize the

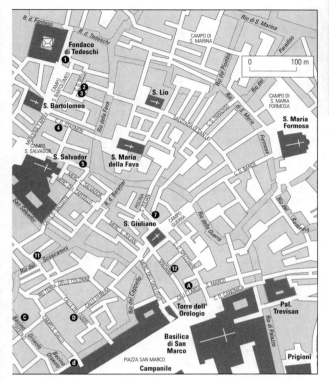

wonder of his continued creativity in extreme old age; a scrap of paper on the rail in front of the picture records the death of the artist on August 25, 1576. Titian also painted the main altarpiece, a *Transfiguration*.

The end of the right transept is filled by the tomb of Caterina Cornaro, one of the saddest figures in Venetian history. Born into one of Venice's pre-eminent families, she became Queen of Cyprus by marriage, and after her husband's death was forced to surrender the strategically crucial island to the doge. On her return home she was led in triumph up the Canal Grande,

as though her abdication had been voluntary, and then was presented with possession of the town of Ásolo as a token of the city's gratitude. She died in 1510, and this tomb erected at the end of the century.

## Campo San Bartolomeo

Terminus of the Mercerie, Campo San Bartolomeo is at its best in the evening, when it's as packed as any bar in town. To show off their new wardrobes the Venetians take themselves off to the Piazza, but Campo San Bartolomeo is the spot to just meet friends and talk. A handful of bars are scattered about, but it's really the atmosphere you come for – unless, that is, you want to join the kids in *McDonald's*, a controversial arrival in Venice. The restoration of the **church of San Bartolomeo** has at last been completed after many years, but access seems to be at the whim of the musicians who use the building for their recitals.

### Campo San Luca and Bacino Orseolo

If the crush of San Bartolomeo is too much for you, you can retire to Campo San Luca (past the front of San Salvatore and straight on), another open-air social centre, where market traders set up their stalls from time to time, temporarily shifting the campo's centre of gravity away from the fast-food outlets. From Campo San Luca, Calle Goldoni is a direct route back to the Piazza, via the Bacino Orseolo – the city's major gondola depot, and one of the few places where you can admire the streamlining and balance of the boats without being hassled by their owners.

### Campo Manin and the Scala del Bovolo

Campo Manin – where, unusually, the most conspicuous building is a modern one, Pier Luigi Nervi's Cassa di Risparmio di Venezia – was enlarged in 1871 to make room for the monument to Daniele Manin, the lawyer who led a revolt against the Austrian occupation in 1848–49. On the wall of the alley on the south side of Campo Manin, a sign

▲ SCALA DEL BOVOLO

directs you to the staircase known as the Scala del Bovolo (a *bovolo* is a snail shell in Venetian dialect). External staircases, developed originally as a way of saving space inside the building, were a common feature of Venetian houses into the sixteenth century, but this specimen, dating from around 1500, is the most flamboyant variation on the theme. You can pay to go up the staircase (April–Oct daily 10am–6pm; Nov–April Sat & Sun 10am–4pm; €3), but the view of it is rather more striking than the view from it.

### The Museo Fortuny

The Museo Fortuny is close at hand, hidden away in a campo you'd never accidentally pass – take either of the bridges out of the Campo Manin, turn first right, and keep going. Born in Catalonia, Mariano Fortuny (1871–1949) is famous chiefly for the body-clinging silk dresses he created, which were so finely pleated that they could be threaded through a wedding ring, it was claimed. However, Fortuny was also a painter, architect, engraver, photographer, theatre designer and sculptor, and the contents of this rickety and atmospheric palazzo reflect his versatility, with ranks of exotic landscapes, come-hither nudes, terracotta portrait busts, stage machinery and so forth. The museum has been undergoing restoration work for many years, but should you find it open you'll probably come out thinking that he's best known for what he was best at, and lamenting the fact that the museum doesn't contain any of the sexy frocks. Design and photography exhibitions are often held here, and as a rule are more interesting than the permanent displays – if the show's good, you'll probably have to queue, as the building is so fragile that only 75 people are allowed in at one time.

## Shops

The Mercerie, connecting the Piazza to Campo San Bartolomeo, is Venice's major shopping district. Here you'll find the Venetian outlets for many of Italy's best-known brands, such as Furla, Mandarina Duck and Gucci, but for distinctly Venetian places you're better off looking on the other side of the Canal Grande, particularly around Campo San Polo – unless, that is, you count Benetton, one of the Veneto's biggest companies, and the occupant of the biggest premises on the *mercerie*.

### Fantoni

Salizzada S. Luca 4119. For the glossiest, weightiest and most expensive art books.

▲ GOLDONI

### Goldoni

Calle dei Fabbri 4742. The best general bookshop in the city; also keeps an array of maps and posters.

### Paolo Olbi

Calle della Mandola 3653. The founder of this shop was largely responsible for the revival of paper marbling; today it sells a whole range of marbled stationery.

### Sansovino

Bacino Orseolo 84. Second only to Fantoni for books on art.

## Cafés and pasticcerie

### Marchini

Calle Spadaria 676. The most delicious and most expensive of Venetian *pasticcerie*, where people come on Sunday morning to buy family treats. Indulge at least once, or take a chocolate mobile phone home as a present.

## Rosa Salva

Campo S. Luca & Merceria S. Salvador. Excellent coffee (the city's best, many would say), very good pastries and pretty good ice creams, served in a slightly surgical ambience.

# Restaurants

## Al Conte Pescaor

Piscina S. Zulian 544 ☎041.522.1483. Closed Sun. Fine (if pricey) little fish restaurant that draws its custom mainly from the locals.

## Le Bistrot de Venise

Calle dei Fabbri 4685. Bar closes at 1am, the kitchen around 30min earlier. This place is done up as a facsimile of a wood-panelled French bistro, but the menu is based on old-style Venetian recipes, both for full meals and *cicheti*. The food and service are variable, to say the least, and the dishes aren't inexpensive, but the atmosphere is the main attraction, as *Le Bistrot* has become something of a community arts centre, with music and poetry events every Tuesday evening from October to May.

## Rosticceria Gislon

Calle della Bissa 5424a. Closed Mon. Downstairs it's a sort of glorified snack bar, serving pizzas and set meals starting at around €7 – the trick is to first grab a place at the long tables along the windows, then order from the counter. Good if you need to refuel quickly and cheaply, but can't face another pizza. There's a less rudimentary restaurant upstairs, where prices are a bit higher for no real increase in quality.

# Bars and snacks

## Alla Botte

Calle della Bissa 5482. Closed Wed evening and all Sun. Well-hidden tiny *bacarò*, just off Campo San Bartolomeo, offering an excellent spread of *cicheti*. Calle della Bissa is one of the most confusing alleyways in Venice – to find *Alla Botte*, take either of the alleys labelled Calle della Bissa (on the east side of the campo), turn first left and go as straight as you can.

## Al Volto

Calle Cavalli 4081. Closed Sun. This dark little bar is an *enoteca* in the true sense of the word – 1300 wines from Italy and elsewhere, 100 of them served by the glass, some cheap, many not; good snacks, too.

## Bácaro Jazz

Salizzada Fondaco dei Tedeschi 5546. Open 11am–2am, closed Wed. A jazz-themed bar that's proving a big hit with cool Venetian kids. The bar food can be dodgy, though.

## Devil's Forest

Calle Stagneri. Daily 10am–1am. The liveliest bar in the vicinity of Campo San Bartolomeo, and a convincing facsimile of a British pub, with a good range of beers and board games in the back.

## Torino

Campo San Luca 4591. Open until 1am, closed Sun & Mon. Lively and loud bar, with live jazz sessions on Wednesdays. Good for sandwiches, or more substantial food at lunchtime.

## Vitae

Calle Sant'Antonio 4118. Open until 2am, closed Sun. Trendy and tiny new bar to the north of Campo Manin, serving superb cocktails.

# San Marco: West of the Piazza

Leaving the Piazza **by the west side** you enter another major shopping district, but one that presents a contrast to the frenetic Mercerie: here the clientele is drawn predominantly from the city's well-heeled or from the five-star tourists staying in the hotels that overlook the end of the Canal Grande – though in recent years it's also become a favourite pitch for African street traders. To a high proportion of visitors, this part of the city is just **the route to the Accademia**, but there are things to see apart from the latest creations from Milan and Paris – the extraordinary Baroque facades of **Santa Maria del Giglio** and **San Moisè**, for instance, or the graceful **Santo Stefano**, which rises at the end of one of the largest and most attractive squares in Venice.

## San Moisè

Daily 3.30–7pm, plus Sun 9am–noon.
San Moisè would be the runaway winner of any poll for the ugliest church in Venice. The church's name means "Saint Moses", the Venetians here following the Byzantine custom of canonizing Old Testament figures, while simultaneously honouring Moisè Venier, who paid for a rebuilding way back in the ninth century. Its delirious facade sculpture was created in 1668 by Heinrich Meyring; and if you think this bloated display of fauna and flora is in questionable taste, wait till you see the miniature mountain he carved as the main altarpiece, representing *Mount Sinai with Moses Receiving the Tablets*.

▲ FACADE OF SAN MOISÈ

## Calle Larga XXII Marzo

If you're looking for an escritoire for your drawing room, an oriental carpet for the reception area, a humble Dutch landscape or a new designer suit, then you'll probably find what you're after on or around the broad Calle Larga XXII Marzo, which begins over the

San Marco: West of the Piazza    PLACES

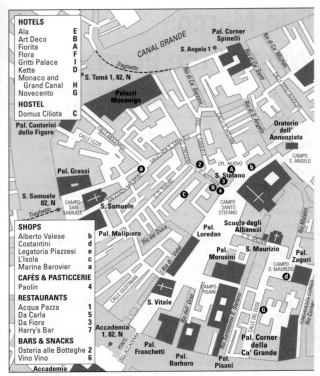

| HOTELS | |
|---|---|
| Ala | E |
| Art Deco | B |
| Fiorita | A |
| Flora | F |
| Gritti Palace | I |
| Kette | D |
| Monaco and Grand Canal | H |
| Novecento | G |
| **HOSTEL** | |
| Domus Ciliota | C |

| SHOPS | |
|---|---|
| Alberto Valese | b |
| Costantini | d |
| Legatoria Piazzesi | e |
| L'Isola | c |
| Marina Barovier | a |
| **CAFÉS & PASTICCERIE** | |
| Paolin | 4 |
| **RESTAURANTS** | |
| Acqua Pazza | 1 |
| Da Carla | 5 |
| Da Fiore | 3 |
| Harry's Bar | 7 |
| **BARS & SNACKS** | |
| Osteria alle Botteghe | 2 |
| Vino Vino | 6 |

canal from San Moisè. Many of the streets off the western side of the Piazza are dedicated to the beautification of the prosperous and their dwellings, with names such as Versace, Gucci, Ferragamo, Prada and Vuitton lurking round every corner.

## La Fenice

Halfway along Calle Larga XXII Marzo, on the right, Calle del Sartor da Veste takes you over a canal and into Campo San Fantin. The square is dominated by the Teatro la Fenice, Venice's oldest and largest theatre. Giannantonio Selva's gaunt Neoclassical design was not deemed a great success on its inauguration on December 26, 1792, but nonetheless very little of the exterior was changed when the place had to be rebuilt after a fire in 1836. Similarly, when La Fenice was again destroyed by fire on the night of January 29, 1996, it was decided to rebuild it as a replica of Selva's theatre: after all, its acoustics were superb and – with a capacity of just 900 people – it had an inspiringly intimate atmosphere. La Fenice saw some significant musical events in the twentieth century – Stravinsky's *The Rake's Progress*

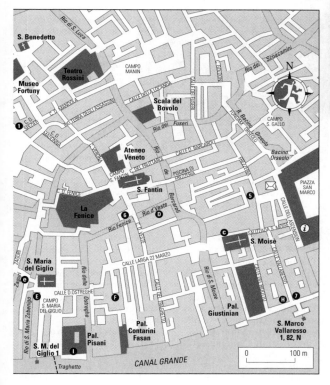

and Britten's *The Turn of the Screw* were both premiered here – but the music scene was more exciting in the nineteenth century, when, in addition to staging the premieres of operas by Rossini, Bellini and Verdi (*Rigoletto* and *La Traviata* both opened here), it became the focal point for protests against the occupying Austrian army. For information on tickets for performances, see p.75.

## Santa Maria del Giglio

Mon–Sat 10am–5pm, Sun 1–5pm. €2 or Chorus Pass – see p.171. Back on the route to the Accademia, another extremely odd church

awaits – Santa Maria del Giglio (Mary of the Lily), more commonly known as Santa Maria Zobenigo, an alternative title derived from the name of the family who founded it in the ninth century. The exterior features not a single unequivocally Christian image: the main statues are of the five Barbaro brothers, who financed the rebuilding of the church in 1678; Virtue, Honour, Fame and Wisdom hover at a respectful distance; and relief maps at eye level depict the towns distinguished with the brothers' presence in the course of their military and diplomatic careers.

▲ FACADE OF SANTA MARIA DEL GIGLIO

reliefs on the facade date from shortly after that.

## Campo Santo Stefano

The church of Santo Stefano closes one end of the spacious Campo Santo Stefano. The campo has an alias – Campo Francesco Morosini – that comes from a former inhabitant of the palazzo at no. 2802, at the Canal Grande end of the square. The last doge to serve as military commander of the Republic (1688–94), Francesco Morosini became a Venetian hero with his victories in the Peloponnese, but is notorious elsewhere as the man who lobbed a missile through the roof of the Parthenon, detonating the Turkish gunpowder barrels that had been stored there.

The **church of Santo Stefano** (Mon–Sat 10am–5pm, Sun 1–5pm; €2 or Chorus Pass – see p.171) is notable for its Gothic doorway and beautiful ship's-keel roof, both of which belong to the last phase of

The interior, full to bursting with devotional pictures and sculptures, overcompensates for the impiety of the exterior.

## San Maurizio and the Scuola degli Albanesi

The tilting campanile of Santo Stefano (see below) looms into view over the vapid and deconsecrated church of San Maurizio, which is sometimes used as an exhibition space. A few metres away, in Calle del Piovan, stands a diminutive building that was once the Scuola degli Albanesi, the confraternity of the city's Albanian community; it was established in 1497 and the

▼ CAMPO SANTO STEFANO

building. The airy and calm interior is one of the most pleasant places in Venice to just sit and think, but it also contains some major works of art, notably in the picture-packed sacristy, where you'll find a *St Lawrence* and a *St Nicholas of Bari* by Bartolomeo Vivarini, a Crucifix by Paolo Veneziano, and a trio of late works by Tintoretto.

### Campo Novo

Nearby Campo Novo was formerly the churchyard of Santo Stefano, and was used as a burial pit during the catastrophic plague of 1630. Such was the volume of corpses interred here that for health reasons the site remained closed to the public from then until 1838.

### Palazzo Pisani

Campiello Pisani, at the back of Morosini's house, is a forecourt to the Palazzo Pisani, one of the biggest houses in the city, and now the Conservatory of Music. Work began on it in the early seventeenth century, continued for over a century, and was at last brought to a halt by the government, who decided that the Pisani, among the city's richest banking families, were getting ideas above their station.

## Shops

As you'd expect, many of the top-flight Italian designers and fashion houses – Versace, Missoni, Krizia, MaxMara, Trussardi, Gucci, Armani, Prada, Valentino, and Dolce e Gabbana (the only ones with a local connection) – are represented in Venice, most of their outlets being clustered to the west of the Piazza, notably in Frezzeria, **Calle**

**Vallaresso** and **Calle Larga XXII Marzo**. The best shops for a range of high fashion are La Coupole (Calle Larga XXII Marzo) and Elysée (Frezzeria and Calle Goldoni).

### Alberto Valese

Campo San Stefano 3471, @www.albertovalese-ebru.com. Open daily. Valese not only produces the most luscious marbled papers in Venice, but also transfers the designs onto silk scarves and a variety of ornaments; the marbling technique he uses is a Turkish process called *ebrû* (meaning cloudy) – hence the alternative name of his shop.

▼ ALBERTO VALESE

### Costantini

Campo San Maurizio 2668a. Large array of *perle veneziane* (glass beads) sold individually, made into jewellery, or by the bag according to weight.

### Legatoria Piazzesi

Campiello della Feltrina 2511. Located near S. Maria Zobenigo, this long-established paper-producer is the last to use the old wooden-block method of printing; stunning hand-printed papers and cards, and a nice line in pocket diaries, too.

### L'Isola

Salizzada S. Moisè 1468. Chiefly a showcase for work by Carlo Moretti, the doyen of modernist Venetian glass artists.

### Marina Barovier

Salizzada San Samuele 3216, ⊛www.barovier.it. Mon–Fri, plus Sat by appointment. This place displays what is perhaps the most inventive and beautiful glass in Venice, and – contrary to appearances – the stuff is for sale, albeit at very high prices.

## Cafés and pasticcerie

### Paolin

Campo S. Stefano 2962. Thought by many to be the makers of the best ice cream in Venice, but some would argue that it's lost ground to *Causin* (see p.86). The outside tables enjoy one of the finest settings in the city.

## Restaurants

### Acqua Pazza

Campo Sant'Angelo 3808, ☎041.277.0688. Closed Mon. Classy restaurant serving good seafood and Neapolitan pizzas (among the best in the city) in an airy, spacious environment.

### Da Carla

Sottoportego Corte Contarina 1535a. Closed Sun. Tiny bar-trattoria hidden down a *sottoportego* off the west side of Frezzeria, a few paces from the Piazza. The battered old sign – reading "Pietro Panizollo" – is a fair indication of the character of this place, which at lunchtimes is packed with workers dropping in for simple pasta dishes and salads.

### Da Fiore

Calle delle Botteghe 3461. Closed Tues. Established in the mid-1990s, this popular mid-range restaurant offers genuine Venetian cuisine in a classy trattoria-style setting. The anteroom is a nice small bar that does very good *cicheti*.

### Harry's Bar

Calle Vallaresso 1323 ☎041.528.5777. Open daily. Often described as the most reliable of the city's gourmet restaurants (*carpaccio* – raw strips of thin beef – was first created here), though there are sceptics who think the place's reputation has more to do with glamour than cuisine. The bar itself is famed in equal measure for its cocktails, its sandwiches and its celebrity-league prices. It's *the* place to sample a *Bellini* (fresh white

peach juice and *prosecco*), which was invented here.

# Bars and snacks

### Osteria alle Botteghe

Calle delle Botteghe 3454. Closed Sun. Sumptuous sandwiches and snacks; most lunchtimes you need a shoehorn to get in the place.

### Vino Vino

Ponte delle Veste 2007. Open 10am–midnight, closed Tues. Very close to the Fenice opera house, this wine bar stocks more than 350 wines. It serves relatively inexpensive meals as well, but the food isn't great.

# Opera

## La Fenice

Campo San Fantin. La Fenice, the third-ranking Italian opera house after Milan's La Scala and Naples' San Carlo, was on the verge of reopening at the time of going to press. Seat prices will probably start at around €20, though you'll pay twice as much for the opening night of a production. The opera season runs from late November to the end of June, punctuated by ballet performances. **Tickets** can be bought at the Fenice box office, or at the Hello Venezia office at Calle dei Fuseri 1810 (℡041.24.24). For up-to-the-minute information, visit Ⓦwww.teatrolafenice.it.

# Dorsoduro

There were not many places among the lagoon's mudbanks where Venice's early settlers could be confident that their dwellings wouldn't slither down into the water, but with Dorsoduro they were on relatively solid ground: the sestiere's name translates as "hard back", and its buildings occupy the largest area of firm silt in the centre of the city. The main draw here is the **Gallerie dell'Accademia**, the city's top art gallery, while the most conspicuous building is the huge church of **Santa Maria della Salute**, the grandest gesture of Venetian Baroque. In terms of artistic contents the Salute takes second place to **San Sebastiano**, the parish church of **Paolo Veronese**. **Giambattista Tiepolo**, the master colourist of a later era, is well represented at the **Scuola Grande dei Carmini**, and for

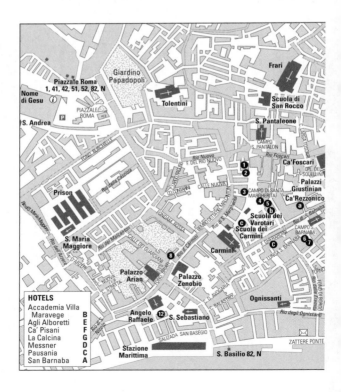

HOTELS
Accademia Villa
  Maravege          B
Agli Alboretti      E
Ca' Pisani          G
La Calcina          F
Messner             D
Pausania            C
San Barnaba         A

an overall view of Tiepolo's cultural milieu there's the **Ca' Rezzonico**, home of Venice's museum of eighteenth-century art and artefacts. Art of the twentieth century is also in evidence – at the **Guggenheim Collection**, which is small yet markedly superior to the city's public collection of modern art in the Ca' Pésaro.

### The Accademia

Mon 8.15am–2pm, Tues–Sun 8.15am–7.15pm. ⊛ www.artive.arti .beniculturali.it. €6.50. The Gallerie dell'Accademia is one of the obligatory tourist sights in Venice, but admissions are restricted to 300 people at a time. Accordingly, if you're visiting in summer and don't want to wait, get there well before the doors open or at about 1pm, when most people are having lunch.

The **first room** of the Accademia's generally chronological arrangement is filled with pieces by the earliest-known individual Venetian painters, Paolo Veneziano and his follower Lorenzo Veneziano. Beyond here, **room 2** is given over to large altarpieces from the late

| SHOPS | |
|---|---|
| Ca' Macana | a |
| La Nave d'Oro | c |
| Libreria della Toletta | d |
| MondoNovo | b |

| CAFÉS & PASTICCERIE | |
|---|---|
| Causin | 4 |
| Il Doge | 5 |
| Nico | 13 |

| RESTAURANTS | |
|---|---|
| Ai Cugnai | 10 |
| Ai Quattro Ferri | 6 |
| Anzolo Raffael | 12 |
| Casin dei Nobili | 7 |
| Da Gianni | 14 |
| La Piscina | 15 |

| BARS & SNACKS | |
|---|---|
| Ai do Draghi | 1 |
| Cantina del Vino già Schiavi | 11 |
| Corner Pub | 9 |
| Da Codroma | 8 |
| Il Caffè | 3 |
| Margaret Du Champ | 4 |

▲ THE ACCADEMIA

fifteenth and early sixteenth centuries, including works by Giovanni Bellini, Cima da Conegliano and **Vittore Carpaccio**. Carpaccio's strange *Crucifixion and Glorification of the Ten Thousand Martyrs of Mount Ararat* is the most gruesome painting in the room, and the most charming is by him too: *The Presentation of Jesus in the Temple*, with its pretty, wingless, lute-playing angel.

The beginnings of the Venetian obsession with the way in which forms are defined by light and the emergence of the characteristically soft and rich Venetian palette are seen in **rooms 3, 4 and 5**, the last two of which are a high point of the Accademia. Outstanding are an exquisite *St George* by Mantegna (c.1466), a series of *Madonnas* and a *Pietà* by Giovanni Bellini, and two pieces by the most mysterious of Italian painters,

Giorgione – his *Portrait of an Old Woman* and the so-called *Tempest* (c.1500).

**Rooms 6 to 8** mark the entry of Tintoretto, Titian, Veronese and Lotto, the heavyweights of the Venetian High Renaissance. These works would be the prize of many other collections, but here they are just appetizers for what's to come in the huge **room 10**, one whole wall of which is needed for *Christ in the House of Levi* by **Paolo Veronese**. Originally called *The Last Supper*, this picture brought down on Veronese the wrath of the Inquisition, who objected to the inclusion of "buffoons, drunkards, Germans, dwarfs, and similar indecencies" in the sacred scene. Veronese's insouciant response was simply to change the title, an emendation that apparently satisfied his critics. Among the works by **Tintoretto** is the painting that made his reputation: *St Mark Freeing a Slave* (1548), showing St Mark's intervention at the execution of a slave who had defied his master by travelling to the Evangelist's shrine. Opposite is **Titian**'s highly charged *Pietà* (1576), painted for his own tomb in the Frari and completed after his death by Palma il Giovane.

In **room 11** a major shift into the eighteenth century occurs, with pieces by **Giambattista Tiepolo**; his contemporaries provide the chief interest of the next section, with works such as Giambattista Piazzetta's extraordinary *The Fortune-Teller*, Guardi's impressionistic views of Venice, Pietro Longhi's documentary interiors and a series of portraits by Rosalba Carriera, one of the very few women shown in the collection.

The vast **room 20** is entirely filled by the cycle of *The Miracles of the Relic of the Cross*, which was produced by various artists between 1494 and 1501, having been commissioned by the Scuola Grande di San Giovanni Evangelista (see p.99) to extol the holy fragment it had held since 1369.

Another remarkable cycle fills **room 21** – Carpaccio's *Story of St Ursula*, painted for the Scuola di Sant'Orsola at San Zanipolo in 1490–94. A superlative exercise in pictorial narrative, the paintings are especially fascinating to the modern viewer as a meticulous record of domestic architecture, costume and the decorative arts in Venice at the close of the fifteenth century. After this room, you leave the Accademia through a door beneath Titian's wonderful *Presentation of the Virgin* (1539), still occupying the space for which it was painted.

## The Guggenheim

10am–6pm, closed Tues; April–Oct open till 10pm on Sat. @ www.guggenheim-venice.it. €8.
The Peggy Guggenheim Collection is installed in the peculiarly modernistic fragment of the quarter-built Palazzo Venier dei Leoni, a bit farther down the Canal Grande.

In the early years of the twentieth century the leading lights of the Futurist movement came here for the parties thrown by the dotty Marchesa Casati, who was fond of stunts like setting wild cats and apes loose in the palazzo garden, among plants sprayed lilac for the occasion. Peggy Guggenheim, a considerably more discerning patron of the arts, moved into the palace in 1949; since her death in 1979 the Guggenheim Foundation has administered the place, and has turned her private collection into one of the city's glossiest museums – and the second most popular after the Accademia. It's

▼ THE GUGGENHEIM

PEGGY GUGGENHEIM COLLECTION

THE SOLOMON R. GUGGENHEIM FOUNDATION

a small but generally top-quality assembly of twentieth-century art and a prime venue for touring exhibitions. In the permanent collection the core pieces include Brancusi's *Bird in Space* and *Maestra*, de Chirico's *Red Tower* and *Nostalgia of the Poet*, Max Ernst's *Robing of the Bride* (Guggenheim was married to Ernst in the 1940s), some of Joseph Cornell's boxes, sculpture by Laurens and Lipchitz, and works by Malevich and Schwitters; other artists include Picasso, Braque, Chagall, Pollock, Duchamp, Giacometti, Picabia and Magritte. Marino Marini's *Angel of the Citadel*, out on the terrace, flaunts his erection at the passing canal traffic; more decorous pieces by Giacometti, Moore, Paolozzi and others are planted in the garden, surrounding Peggy Guggenheim's burial place.

▲ SANTA MARIA DELLA SALUTE

## Santa Maria della Salute

Daily 9am–noon & 3–5.30pm. In 1630–31 Venice was devastated by a plague that exterminated nearly 95,000 of the lagoon's population – one person in three. In October 1630 the Senate decreed that a new church would be dedicated to Mary if the city were saved, and the result was Santa Maria della Salute (*salute* meaning "health" and "salvation"). Resting on a platform of more than 100,000 wooden piles, the Salute took half a century to build; its architect, **Baldassare Longhena**, was only 26 years old when his proposal was accepted and lived just long

enough to see it finished, in 1681.

Each year on November 21 (the Feast of the Presentation of the Virgin) the Signoria processed from San Marco to the Salute for a service of thanksgiving, crossing the Canal Grande on a pontoon bridge laid from Santa Maria del Giglio. The Festa della Madonna della Salute is still a major event in the Venetian calendar.

The form of the Salute owes much to the plan of Palladio's Redentore (see p.150) – the obvious model for a dramatically sited votive church – and to the repertoire of Marian symbolism. The octagonal plan and eight facades allude to the eight-pointed Marian star, for example, while the huge dome represents Mary's crown and the centralized plan is a conventional symbol of the Virgin's womb. Less arcane symbolism is at work on the high altar, where the Virgin and Child rescue Venice (kneeling woman) from the plague (old woman); in attendance are SS. Mark and Lorenzo Giustiniani, first Patriarch of Venice.

The most notable paintings in the Salute are the Titian pieces brought from the suppressed church of Santo Spirito in 1656, and now displayed in the sacristy (€1.50). Tintoretto has included himself in the dramatis personae of his *Marriage at Cana* (1561) – he's the first Apostle on the left.

### The Záttere and the Gesuati

Known collectively as the **Záttere**, the sequence of waterfront pavements between the Punta della Dogana and the Stazione Maríttima, are now a popular place for a stroll or an al fresco pizza, but were formerly the place where most of the bulky goods coming into Venice

▼ THE GESUATI

were unloaded onto floating rafts called *záttere*.

The first building to break your stride for is the church of the **Gesuati** or Santa Maria del Rosario (Mon–Sat 10am–5pm, Sun 1–5pm; €2, or Chorus Pass). Rebuilt in 1726–43, about half a century after the church was taken over from the order of the Gesuati by the Dominicans, this was the first church designed by Giorgio Massari, an architect who often worked with Giambattista Tiepolo. Tiepolo painted the first altarpiece on the right, *The Virgin with SS. Catherine of Siena, Rose and Agnes* (c.1740), and the three magnificent ceiling panels of *Scenes from the Life of St Dominic* (1737–39), which are seen to best effect in the afternoon. The third altar on this side of the church is adorned with a painting of *SS. Vincent Ferrer, Giacinto and Luigi Beltran* by Tiepolo's principal forerunner, Giambattista Piazzetta; opposite, the first altar has Sebastiano Ricci's *Pius V with SS. Thomas and Peter Martyr* (1739), completing the church's array of Rococo propaganda on behalf of the exalted figures of Dominican orthodoxy, followed by a tragically intense *Crucifixion* by Tintoretto (c.1555) on the third altar.

### The squero di San Trovaso

Ten thousand gondolas operated on the canals of sixteenth-century Venice, when they were the standard form of transport around the city; nowadays the tourist trade is pretty well all that sustains the city's fleet of around five hundred gondolas, which provide steady employment for a few **squeri**, as the gondola yards are called. A display in the Museo Storico

Navale (see p.128) takes you through the construction of a gondola, but no abstract demonstration can equal the fascination of a working yard, and the most public one in Venice is the squero di San Trovaso, on the Záttere side of San Trovaso church. The San Trovaso is the oldest *squero* still functioning – established in the seventeenth century, it looks rather like an alpine farmhouse, a reflection of the architecture of the Dolomite villages from which many of Venice's gondola-builders once came.

### San Trovaso

Mon–Sat 3–6pm. Don't bother consulting your dictionary of saints for the dedicatee of San Trovaso church – the name's a baffling dialect version of Santi Gervasio e Protasio. Since its tenth-century foundation the church has had a chequered history, falling down once, and twice being destroyed by fire; this is the fourth incarnation, built in 1584–1657.

Venetian folklore has it that this church was the only neutral ground between the Nicolotti and the Castellani, the two factions in to which the working-class citizens of the city were divided – the former, coming from the west and north of the city, were named after the church of San Nicolò dei Mendicoli (see p.83), the latter, from the sestieri of Dorsoduro, San Marco and Castello, took their name from San Pietro di Castello. The rivals celebrated intermarriages and other services here, but are said to have entered and departed by separate doors.

Inside, San Trovaso is spacious and somewhat characterless, but

▲ SAN TROVASO

it does boast a pair of fine paintings by Tintoretto: *The Temptation of St Anthony* and *The Last Supper*. The former is in the chapel to the left of the high altar, with *St Crysogonus on Horseback* by Michele Giambono (c.1450), Venice's main practitioner of the International Gothic style; the latter is in the chapel at ninety degrees to the first one.

### San Sebastiano

Mon–Sat 10am–5pm, Sun 1–5pm – but often closed Sun in winter. €2 or Chorus Pass – see p.171. At the end of the Záttere the barred gates of the Stazione Maríttima deflect you away from the waterfront and towards the church of San Sebastiano. The parish church of **Paolo Veronese**, it contains a group of resplendent paintings by him that gives it a place in his career comparable to that of San Rocco in the career of Tintoretto. Veronese was still in his twenties when he was asked to paint the ceiling of the sacristy with a *Coronation of the Virgin* and the *Four Evangelists* (1555); once that commission had been carried out, he decorated the nave ceiling with *Scenes from the Life of St Esther*. His next project, the dome of the chancel, was later destroyed, but the sequence he and his brother Benedetto then painted on the walls of the church and the nun's choir at the end of the 1550s has survived in pretty good shape. In the following decade he executed the last of the pictures, those on the organ shutters and around the high altar – on the left, *St Sebastian Leads SS. Mark and Marcellian to Martyrdom*, and on the right *The Second Martyrdom of St Sebastian* (the customarily depicted torture by arrows didn't kill him). Other riches include a late **Titian** of *St Nicholas* (on the left wall of the first chapel on the right), and the early sixteenth-century majolica pavement in the chapel to the left of the chancel – in front of which is Veronese's tomb slab.

## Angelo Raffaele

Daily 8am–noon & 4–6pm. At the back of San Sebastiano, the seventeenth-century church of Angelo Raffaele is instantly recognizable by the two huge war memorials blazoned on the canal facade. Inside, the organ loft above the entrance on the canal side is decorated with *Scenes from the Life of St Tobias* (accompanied, as ever, by his little dog), painted by one or other of the Guardi brothers (nobody's sure which). Although small in scale, the free brushwork and imaginative composition make the panels among the most charming examples of Venetian Rococo, a fascinating counterpoint to the grander visions of Giambattista Tiepolo, the Guardis' brother-in-law.

## San Nicolò dei Mendicoli

Daily 10am–noon & 4–6pm. Although it's located on the edge of the city, the church of San Nicolò dei Mendicoli is one of Venice's oldest, said to have been founded in the seventh century. Its long history was reflected in the fact that it gave its name to the **Nicolotti faction**, whose titular head, the so-called *Gastaldo* or the *Doge dei Nicolotti*, was elected by the parishioners and then honoured by a ceremonial greeting from the Republic's doge.

The church has been rebuilt and altered at various times, and was last restored in the 1970s, when Nic Roeg used it as a setting for *Don't Look Now*. In essence, however, its shape is still that of the Veneto-Byzantine structure raised here in the twelfth century, the date of its rugged campanile. The other conspicuous feature of the exterior is the fifteenth-century porch, a type of construction once common in Venice, and often used here as makeshift accommodation for penurious nuns. The interior is a miscellany of periods and styles. Parts of the apse and the columns of the nave go back to the twelfth century, but the darkened gilded woodwork that gives the interior its rather overcast appearance was installed late in the sixteenth century, as were most of the paintings.

## Campo Santa Margherita and the Carmini

The vast, elongated **Campo Santa Margherita**, ringed by houses that date back as far as the fourteenth century, is the social heart of Dorsoduro, many of whose inhabitants come here daily to stock up at the market stalls. Students from the nearby university hang out in the campo's bars, and the place as a whole has a vaguely alternative feel.

Just off Campo Santa Margherita's southwest tip is the **Scuola Grande dei Carmini** (April–Oct Mon–Sat 9am–6pm, Sun 9am–1pm; Nov–March Mon–Sat 9am–4pm, Sun 9am–1pm; €5), once the Venetian base of the Carmelites. Originating in Palestine towards the close of the twelfth century, the Carmelites blossomed during the Counter-Reformation, when they became the shock-troops through whom the cult of the Virgin could be disseminated, as a response to the inroads of Protestantism. As happened elsewhere in Europe, the Venetian Carmelites became immensely wealthy, and in the 1660s they called in an architect – probably Longhena – to redesign the property they had acquired. The core of this complex, which in 1767 was raised to the status of a Scuola Grande (see p.98), is now effectively a showcase for the art of **Giambattista Tiepolo**, who in the 1740s painted the wonderful ceiling of the upstairs hall.

## Santa Maria del Carmelo

The **Carmini** church, or Santa Maria del Carmelo (Mon–Sat 7.30am–noon & 2.30–7pm), is a collage of architectural styles, with a sixteenth-century facade, a Gothic side doorway which preserves several Byzantine fragments, and a fourteenth-century basilican interior. A dull series of Baroque paintings

▲ SANTA MARIA DEL CARMELO

illustrating the history of the Carmelite order covers a lot of space inside, but the second altar on the right has a *Nativity* by Cima da Conegliano (before 1510), and Lorenzo Lotto's *St Nicholas of Bari* (1529) – featuring what Bernard Berenson ranked as one of the most beautiful landscapes in all Italian art – hangs on the opposite side of the nave.

## The Ponte dei Pugni and San Barnaba

Cutting down the side of the Carmini church takes you over the Rio di San Barnaba, along which a fondamenta runs to the church of San Barnaba. Just before the end of the fondamenta you pass the **Ponte**

**dei Pugni**, one of several bridges with this name. Originally built without parapets, they were the sites of ritual battles between the Castellani and Nicolotti; this one is inset with marble footprints marking the starting positions. Pugilists have now been replaced by tourists taking shots of the photogenic San Barnaba grocery barge moored at the foot of the bridge.

The huge, damp-ridden **San Barnaba** church (daily 9.30am–12.30pm & 2.30–7pm), built in 1749, has a trompe l'oeil ceiling painting of *St Barnabas in Glory* by Constantino Cedini, a follower of Tiepolo. Despite recent restoration, the ceiling is being restored again because of moisture damage.

## Ca' Rezzonico

Wed–Sun: April–Oct 10am–5pm; Nov–March 9am–4pm. €6.50. The **Museo del Settecento Veneziano** – the Museum of the Venetian Eighteenth Century – spreads through most of the enormous Ca' Rezzonico, a palazzo which the city authorities bought in 1934 specifically as a home for the museum. It's never been one of the most popular of Venice's museums, but a recently completed renovation might go some way to rectifying its unjustified neglect.

A man in constant demand in the early part of the eighteenth century was the Belluno sculptor-cum-woodcarver Andrea Brustolon, much of whose output consisted of wildly elaborate pieces of furniture, exemplified by the stuff on show in the **Brustolon Room**. The less fervid imaginations of **Giambattista Tiepolo** and his son **Giandomenico** are introduced in **room 2** with the ceiling fresco celebrating Ludovico Rezzonico's marriage into the hugely powerful Savorgnan family in 1758. Beyond **room 4**, with its array of pastels by Rosalba Carriera, you come to two other Tiepolo ceilings, enlivening the rooms overlooking the Canal Grande on each side of the main portego – an *Allegory of Merit* by Giambattista and Giandomenico, and *Nobility and Virtue Triumphing over Perfidy*, a solo effort by the father.

▼ CA' REZZONICO

In the portego of the **second floor** hang the only two canal views by **Canaletto** on show in public galleries in Venice. The next suite of rooms contains the museum's most engaging paintings – Giandomenico Tiepolo's sequence of frescoes from the Villa Zianigo near Mestre, the Tiepolo family home. There then follows a succession of rooms with delightful portraits and depictions of everyday Venetian life by Francesco Guardi (including high-society recreation in the parlour of San Zaccaria's convent) and Pietro Longhi, whose artlessly candid work – such as a version of the famous *Rhinoceros* – has more than enough curiosity value to make up for its shortcomings in execution.

The low-ceilinged rooms of the **third and fourth floors** house a less than thrilling private donation of Venetian art from the fifteenth to twentieth centuries, but the main point of clambering upstairs (apart from the tremendous view across the rooftops) is to see the **pharmacy**, a sequence of wood-panelled rooms heavily stocked with ceramic jars and glass bottles.

## Shops

### Ca' Macana
Calle delle Botteghe 3172. Open daily. Huge mask shop, with perhaps the biggest stock in the city; has another branch on the other side of Campo San Barnaba, at Barbaria delle Tole 1169.

### La Nave d'Oro
Campo S. Margherita 3664. Closed Mon morning. This is the city's best outlet for local wines, selling not just bottles but also draught Veneto wine to take out. Other branches at Calle del Mondo Novo, Castello 5786 (closed Wed afternoon), Rio Terrà S. Leonardo, Cannaregio 1370 (closed Wed afternoon), and Via Lépanto, Lido 241.

### Libreria della Toletta
Sacca della Toletta 1214. Sells reduced-price books, mainly in Italian, but some dual language and translations. Another branch on the opposite side of the street sells art books, including some bargains.

### MondoNovo
Rio Terrà Canal 3063. This mask workshop, located just off Campo S. Margherita, is perhaps the most imaginative in the city, producing everything from ancient Greek tragic masks to portraits of Richard Wagner.

## Cafés and pasticcerie

### Causin
Campo S. Margherita 2996. Closed Sun. Excellent homemade ice cream at this long-established café, which has seating on the campo.

### Il Doge
Campo S. Margherita 3058. Open daily till midnight, until 2am June–Sept. Closed Nov & Dec. Well-established café-gelateria. Like *Causin*, it ranks among the city's best.

### Nico
Záttere ai Gesuati 922. Closed Thurs. Celebrated for an artery-clogging creation called a *gianduiotto* – ask for one *da passeggio* (to take out) and you'll be given a paper cup with a

▲ NICO

block of praline ice cream drowned in whipped cream.

# Restaurants

### Ai Cugnai

Piscina del Forner 857. Closed Mon. Remarkably unspoilt considering it's just a few yards to the east of the Accademia, this is a very popular and reasonable little trattoria, run by a family of gregarious Venetian senior citizens. Orders are memorized and can become scrambled between table and kitchen, but that's part of the fun. Supposed to close at 9pm, but keeps going if the mood takes them.

### Ai Quattro Ferri

Calle Lunga S. Barnaba 2754/a ☎041.520.6978. Closed Sun. Highly recommended osteria just off Campo S. Barnaba, with delicious *cicheti* and an inexpensive menu that changes daily. No credit cards. Booking essential in high season.

### Anzolo Raffael

Campo Angelo Raffaele 1722. Closed Mon lunchtime and all day Tues July–Oct. Unpretentious parish restaurant tucked in a corner of the sestiere where few tourists venture – except to come here. The small menu includes first-class fish. Might close as early as 9pm, depending on how they feel. No credit cards.

### Casin dei Nobili

Calle Lombardo 2765. Closed Mon. Popular with both locals and tourists, this place serves excellent (and large) pizzas plus a varied menu that includes local specialities such as eel. Good two-course menu with water and wine for €24. Separate dining area for smokers. *Casin* or *casino* means brothel, as you'll gather from the place mats – not to be confused with *casinò*, which means casino.

### Da Gianni

Záttere ai Gesuati 918a. Closed Wed. Nicely sited restaurant-pizzeria, right by the Záttere vaporetto stop and slightly better than the nearby Alle Záttere. No credit cards.

### La Piscina

Záttere ai Gesuati 780 ☎041.520.6466. Closed Mon. Stretching onto the waterfront outside the *Calcina* hotel, to which it's attached, this is one of the most enjoyable restaurants in Dorsoduro. The service is excellent, the menu of salads and light Mediterranean dishes sets it apart from its neighbours, and the view of Giudecca from the terrace is wonderful.

## Bars and snacks

### Ai Do Draghi

Campo S. Margherita 3665. Open 8am–2am. Taking its name from the two dragons on the wall opposite, this is a tiny, friendly café-bar, with a good range of wines. The back room exhibits the work of local photographers.

### Cantina del Vino già Schiavi

Fondamenta Nani 992. Open till 8.30pm, closed Sun. Great bar and wine shop opposite San Trovaso

– do some sampling before you buy. Excellent *cicheti*, too.

### Corner Pub

Calle della Chiesa 684. Open till at least 12.30am, closed Mon. Very close to the Guggenheim, this place usually has a few arty foreigners in attendance, but they are always outnumbered by the locals.

### Da Codroma

Fondamenta Briati 2540. Open till midnight, closed Sun. The kind of place where you could sit for an hour or two with a beer and a book and feel comfortable. Popular with students from the nearby University of Architecture. Occasional poetry readings and live jazz.

### Il Caffè

Campo S. Margherita 2963. Open till 2am, closed Sun. Known as *Caffè Rosso* for its big red sign, this inviting, old-fashioned café-bar is a student favourite, with chairs out on the square and live jazz, blues or rock on Thursdays.

### Margaret Du Champ

Campo S. Margherita 3019. Open till 2am, closed Tues. Much the classiest of the campo's late bars, with a self-consciously chic ambience.

▼ MARGARET DU CHAMP

# San Polo and Santa Croce

As far as the day-to-day life of Venice is concerned, the focal points of the San Polo and Santa Croce sestieri are the sociable open space of **Campo San Polo** and the **Rialto** area, once the commercial heart of the Republic and still the home of a **market** that's famous far beyond the boundaries of the city. The bustle of the stalls and the unspoilt bars used by the porters are a good antidote to cultural overload. Nobody, however, should miss the extraordinary pair of buildings in the southern part of San Polo: the colossal Gothic church of **the Frari**, embellished with three of Venice's finest altarpieces, and the **Scuola Grande di San Rocco**, decorated with an unforgettable cycle of paintings by Tintoretto.

In the northern part of the district, Venice's erratically open **modern art, oriental and natural history museums** are clustered together on the bank of the Canal Grande: the first two collections occupy one of the city's most magnificent palaces, while the third is installed in the former headquarters of the Turkish merchants. As ever, numerous treasures are also scattered among the minor churches – for example in **San Cassiano**, **San Simeone Grande** and **San Pantaleone**. Lastly, if you're in search of a spot in which to sit for an hour and just watch the world go by, head for the **Campo San Giacomo dell'Orio**, one of Venice's more spacious and tranquil squares.

## The Rialto

As the political centre of Venice grew around San Marco, the Rialto became the commercial area. In the twelfth century Europe's first state bank was opened here, and the financiers of this quarter were to be the heavyweights of the international currency exchanges for the next three hundred years and more. And through the markets of the Rialto Venice earned a reputation as the bazaar of Europe. Trading had been going on here for over four hundred years when, in the winter of 1514, a fire destroyed everything in the area except the church. Reconstruction began almost straight away: the **Fabbriche Vecchie** (the arcaded buildings along the Ruga degli Orefici and around the Campo San Giacomo) were finished five years after the fire, with Sansovino's **Fabbriche Nuove**

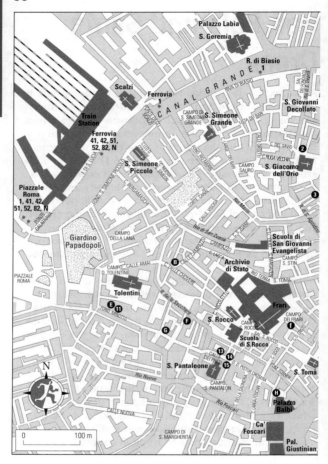

(running along the Canal Grande) following about thirty years later.

Today's Rialto market is tamer than that of Venice at its peak, but it's still one of the liveliest spots in the city, and one of the few places where it's possible to stand in a crowd and hear nothing but Italian spoken. You'll find fruit sellers, vegetable stalls, cheese kiosks, a number of good *alimentari* and some fine old-fashioned bars here. In short, if you can't find something to excite your taste buds around the Rialto, they must be in a sorry state. The Rialto market is open Monday to Saturday 8am to 1pm, with a few stalls opening again in the late afternoon; the **Pescheria** (fish market) – of no practical interest to picnickers but a sight

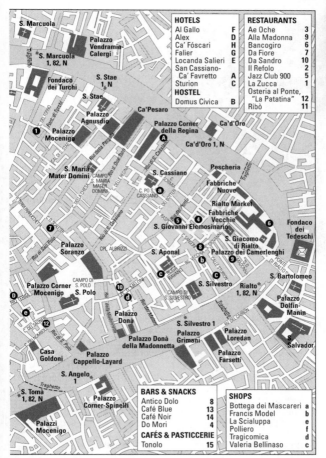

| HOTELS | |
| --- | --- |
| Al Gallo | F |
| Alex | D |
| Ca' Fóscari | H |
| Falier | G |
| Locanda Salieri | E |
| San Cassiano- | |
| Ca' Favretto | A |
| Sturion | C |
| HOSTEL | |
| Domus Civica | B |

| RESTAURANTS | |
| --- | --- |
| Ae Oche | 3 |
| Alla Madonna | 9 |
| Bancogiro | 6 |
| Da Fiore | 7 |
| Da Sandro | 10 |
| Il Refolo | 2 |
| Jazz Club 900 | 5 |
| La Zucca | 1 |
| Osteria al Ponte, | |
| "La Patatina" | 12 |
| Ribò | 11 |

| BARS & SNACKS | |
| --- | --- |
| Antico Dolo | 8 |
| Café Blue | 13 |
| Café Noir | 14 |
| Do Mori | 4 |
| CAFÉS & PASTICCERIE | |
| Tonolo | 15 |

| SHOPS | |
| --- | --- |
| Bottega dei Mascareri | a |
| Francis Model | b |
| La Scialuppa | e |
| Polliero | f |
| Tragicomica | d |
| Valeria Bellinaso | c |

not to be missed – is closed on
Monday as well.

Venetian legend asserts that
the city was founded at noon
on Friday, March 25, 421; from
the same legend derives the
claim that the church of **San
Giacomo di Rialto** (Mon–Sat
9.30–noon & 4–6pm) was
consecrated in that year, and is
thus the oldest church in Venice.
Whatever the truth of the

matter, parts of the present
structure date from a rebuilding
in 1071 – the interior's six
columns of ancient Greek
marble have eleventh-century
Veneto-Byzantine capitals – and
it seems likely that the
reconstruction of the church
prompted the establishment of
the market here.

On the opposite side of the
campo from the church

▲ DELIVERIES AT RIALTO MARKET

crouches a stone figure known as the **Gobbo di Rialto** or the Rialto hunchback. It supports a granite platform from which state proclamations were read simultaneously with their announcement from the Pietra del Bando, beside San Marco; it had another role as well – certain wrongdoers were sentenced to run the gauntlet, stark naked, from the Piazza to the Gobbo.

### San Cassiano

The barn-like church of San Cassiano (daily 9am–noon & 5–7pm) is a building you're bound to pass as you wander out of the Rialto. The thirteenth-century campanile is the only appealing aspect of the exterior, but inside there are three fine paintings by **Tintoretto**: *The Resurrection*, *The Descent into Limbo* and *The Crucifixion*. The third is one of the most startling pictures in Venice – centred on the ladder on which the executioners

stand, it's painted as though the observer were lying in the grass at the foot of the Cross.

**Campo San Cassiano** was the site of the first public opera house in the world – it opened in 1636, at the peak of Monteverdi's career. Long into the following century Venice's opera houses were among the most active in Europe; around five hundred works received their first performances here in the first half of the eighteenth century.

### Santa Maria Mater Domini

The small Campo Santa Maria Mater Domini would have to be included in any anthology of the hidden delights of Venice; it's a typically Venetian miscellany – a thirteenth-century house (the Casa Zane), a few ramshackle Gothic houses, an assortment of stone reliefs of indeterminate age, a fourteenth-century well-head in the centre, a couple of bars, and an ironsmith's workshop tucked into one corner. The **church** of Santa Maria Mater Domini (Tues–Fri 10am–noon), an early sixteenth-century building, boasts an endearing *Martyrdom of St Christina* by Vincenzo Catena.

### Ca' Pésaro

The Ca' Pésaro was bequeathed to the city at the end of the nineteenth century by the Duchessa Felicità Bevilacqua La Masa, who stipulated in her will that it should provide studio and exhibition space for impoverished young artists. Subsequent machinations put paid to the Duchess's enlightened plans, and in place of the intended living arts centre the city acquired the **Galleria Internazionale d'Arte Moderna** (Tues–Sun:

▲ CA' PÉSARO

10am–5pm, Sun 1–5pm; €2 or Chorus Pass – see p.171). In the chancel there's a series of paintings from the beginning of the eighteenth century, the pick of which are *The Martyrdom of St James the Great* by Piazzetta (low on the left), *The Liberation of St Peter* by Sebastiano Ricci (same row) and *The Martyrdom of St Bartholomew* by Giambattista Tiepolo (opposite). Exhibitions and concerts are often held in San Stae, and exhibitions are also held from time to time in the diminutive building alongside, the early seventeenth-century **Scuola dei Battioro e Tiraoro** (Goldsmiths' Guild).

April–Oct 10am–6pm; Nov–March 10am–5; €5.50, including the Museo Orientale, or Museum Pass – see p.171). Most of the stuff in this collection is modern only in the chronological sense of the term: pieces bought from the Biennale formed the foundation of the collection, and in its early years the Biennale was a celebration of all that was most conservative in European art. This is one of the city's weaker museums, and the same goes for the **Museo Orientale**, on the palace's top floor, whose jumble of lacquer work, armour, screens, weaponry and so forth is not likely to appeal to the uninitiated.

## San Stae and the Scuola dei Battioro e Tiraoro

Calle Pésaro takes you over the Rio della Rioda to the seventeenth-century church of **San Stae** (Mon–Sat

▼ EXTERIOR OF SAN STAE

## Palazzo Mocenigo

Tues–Sun: April–Oct 10am–5pm; Nov–March 10am–4pm. €4 or Museum Pass – see p.171. Halfway down the alley flanking San Stae is the early seventeenth-century Palazzo Mocenigo, now home to a centre for the study of textiles and clothing. The library and archive of the study centre occupy part of the building, but a substantial portion of the *piano nobile* is open to the public, and there are few Venetian interiors of this date that have been so meticulously preserved. The main room is decorated with workaday portraits of various Mocenigo men, while the rooms to the side are full of miscellaneous pictures, antique furniture, Murano chandeliers, and display cases of dandified clothing and cobweb-fine lacework. The curtains are kept closed to protect such delicate items as floral silk stockings, silvery padded waistcoats, and an extraordinarily embroidered outfit once worn by what must have been the best-dressed five-year-old in town.

## San Giovanni Decollato

Mon–Sat 10am–noon. The signposted route to the train station passes the deconsecrated church of San Giovanni Decollato, or San Zan Degolà in dialect – it means "St John the Beheaded". Established in the opening years of the eleventh century, it has retained its layout through several alterations; the columns and capitals of the nave date from the first century of its existence, and parts of its fragmentary frescoes (at the east end) could be of the same age. Some of the paintings are certainly thirteenth century, and no other church in Venice has

frescoes that predate them. The church also has one of the city's characteristic ship's-keel ceilings.

## The Museo di Storia Naturale

The **Museo di Storia Naturale** is right by the church, in the **Fondaco dei Turchi**, which was once a hostel-cum-warehouse for Turkish traders. Top-billing exhibits are the remains of a 37-foot-long ancestor of the crocodile and an Ouranosaurus, both dug up in the Sahara in 1973; of stricter relevance to Venetian life is the display relating to the lagoon's marine life, and a pre-Roman boat dredged from the silt. However, in recent years the building has been undergoing a major restoration, and at the moment only the aquarium and dinosaur room are open (Sat & Sun 10am–4pm; free).

## San Giacomo dell'Orio

Standing in a lovely campo which, despite its size, you could easily miss if you weren't looking for it, San Giacomo dell'Orio (Mon–Sat 10am–5pm, Sun 1–5pm; €2 or Chorus Pass – see p.171) is an ancient and atmospheric church. Founded in the ninth century (the shape of the apse betrays its Byzantine origins), it was rebuilt in 1225 and remodelled on numerous subsequent occasions, notably when its ship's-keel roof was added in the fourteenth century. Several fine paintings are to be seen here. The main altarpiece, *Madonna and Four Saints*, was painted by Lorenzo Lotto in 1546, shortly before he left the city complaining that the Venetians had not treated him fairly; the Crucifix that hangs in the air in front of it is attributed to Paolo Veneziano. In the left

▲ SAN GIACOMO DELL'ORIO

1317 by Marco Romano, but some experts doubt that the sculpture can be that old, as nothing else of that date bears comparison with it. Originating in the tenth century, the church has often been rebuilt – most extensively in the eighteenth century, when the city sanitation experts, anxious about the condition of the plague victims who had been buried under the flagstones in the 1630 epidemic, ordered the whole floor to be relaid.

## San Polo

South of the Rialto, Ruga Vecchia San Giovanni constitutes the first leg of the right bank's nearest equivalent to the Mercerie of San Marco, a reasonably straight chain of shop-lined alleyways that is interrupted by **Campo San Polo**, the largest square in Venice after the Piazza. In earlier times it was the site of weekly markets and occasional fairs, as well as being used as a parade ground and bullfighting

transept there's an altarpiece by Paolo Veronese, and there's a fine set of pictures from Veronese's workshop on the ceiling of the new sacristy. The old sacristy is a showcase for the art of Palma il Giovane, whose cycle in celebration of the Eucharist covers the walls and part of the ceiling.

### San Simeone Profeta

Mon–Sat 9am–noon & 5–6.30pm. San Giacomo dell'Orio is plumb in the middle of an extensive residential district, much of which is as close to bland as you can get in Venice. Don't, though, overlook the church of San Simeone Profeta (or Grande) – remarkable for its reclining effigy of Saint Simeon (to the left of the chancel), a luxuriantly bearded, larger than life-size figure, whose half-open mouth disturbingly creates the impression of the moment of death. According to its inscription, it was sculpted in

▼ SAN POLO

arena. And on one occasion Campo San Polo was the scene of a bloody act of political retribution: on February 26, 1548, Lorenzaccio de'Medici, having fled Florence after murdering the deranged Duke Alessandro (a distant relative and former friend), was murdered here by assassins sent by Duke Cosimo I, Alessandro's successor.

The bleak interior of **San Polo church** (Mon–Sat 10am–5pm, Sun 1–5pm; €2 or Chorus Pass – see p.171) is worth a visit for a superior *Last Supper* by Tintoretto (on the left as you enter) and a cycle of the *Stations of the Cross* (*Via Crucis*) by Giandomenico Tiepolo in the Oratory of the Crucifix, painted when the artist was only twenty.

## Casa Goldoni

Mon–Sat 10am–5pm, Nov–March closes 4pm. €2.50 or Museum Pass – see p.171. The fifteenth-century Palazzo Centani, in Calle dei Nomboli, was the birthplace of Carlo Goldoni (1707–93), the playwright who transformed the *commedia dell'arte* from a vehicle for semi-improvised clowning into a medium for sharp political observation. Goldoni's plays are still the staple of theatrical life in Venice, and there's no risk of running out of material – allegedly, he once bet a friend that he could produce one play a week for a whole year, and won. Goldoni's home now houses a theatre studies institute and the **Museo Goldoni**, a small collection of first editions, autograph papers and theatrical paraphernalia, including some eighteenth-century marionettes and a miniature theatre.

## Santa Maria Gloriosa dei Frari

Mon–Sat 9am–6pm, Sun 1–6pm. €2 or Chorus Pass – see p.171. Santa Maria Gloriosa dei Frari – abbreviated to **the Frari** – was founded by the Franciscans around 1250, not long after the death of their founder, but almost no sooner was the first church completed (in 1338) than work began on a vast replacement, a project which took well over a hundred years. The campanile, one of the city's landmarks and the tallest after San Marco's, was finished in 1396.

You're unlikely to fall in love at first sight with this mountain of brick, but the outside of the church is a misleadingly dull prelude to an astounding interior. Apart from the Accademia and the Salute, the Frari is the only building in

▼ TITIAN'S ASSUMPTION

Venice with more than a single first-rate work by **Titian**, and one of these – the **Assumption** – you'll see right away, as it soars over the high altar. It's a piece of compositional and colouristic bravura for which there was no precedent in Venetian art (no previous altarpiece had emphasized the vertical axis), and the other Titian

▲ BELLINI'S ALTARPIECE

masterpiece here, the **Madonna di Ca' Pésaro** (on the left wall, between the third and fourth columns), was equally innovative in its displacement of the figure of the Virgin from the centre of the picture. Other paintings to look out for are Bartolomeo Vivarini's *St Mark Enthroned* (in the Cappella Corner, at the end of the left transept), Alvise Vivarini's *St Ambrose and other Saints* (in the adjoining chapel, where you'll also find the grave of Monteverdi), and, above all, **Giovanni Bellini**'s serene and solemn *Madonna and Child with SS. Nicholas of Bari, Peter, Mark and Benedict*, in the sacristy.

Apart from its paintings, the Frari is also remarkable for Donatello's luridly naturalistic wooden statue of *St John the Baptist* (in the chapel to the right of the transept), the beautiful fifteenth-century monks' choir, and its wealth of extravagant **tombs**. Two of the finest monuments flank the Titian *Assumption*: on the left is the proto-Renaissance tomb of

Doge Niccolò Tron, by Antonio Rizzo and assistants (1476); on the right, the more archaic and chaotic tomb of Doge Francesco Fóscari, carved shortly after Fóscari's death in 1457 (after 34 years as doge) by Antonio and Paolo Bregno.

Against the right-hand wall of the nave stands the house-sized **monument to Titian**, built in the mid-nineteenth century on the supposed place of his burial. The artist died in 1576, in around his ninetieth year, a casualty of the plague; such was the esteem in which Titian was held, he was the only victim to be allowed a church burial in the course of the outbreak. The marble pyramid on the opposite side of the church is the **Mausoleum of Canova**, erected by pupils of the sculptor, following a design he himself had made for the tombs of Titian and Maria Christina of Austria. Finally, you can't fail to notice what is surely the most grotesque monument in the city, the tomb of **Doge**

**Giovanni Pésaro** (1669), held aloft by gigantic ragged-trousered Moors and decomposing corpses.

## The Scuola Grande di San Rocco

Daily: April–Oct 9am–5.30pm; Nov–March 10am–4pm. €5.50, €4 with Venice Card. Unless you've been to the Scuola Grande di San Rocco you can't properly appreciate the achievement of **Tintoretto**. Ruskin called it "one of the three most precious buildings in Italy", and it's not difficult to understand why he resorted to such hyperbole. (His other votes were for the Sistine Chapel and the Campo Santo at Pisa – the latter was virtually ruined in World War II.) The unremitting concentration and restlessness of Tintoretto's paintings won't inspire unqualified enthusiasm in everyone, but even those who prefer their art at a lower voltage should find this an overwhelming experience.

From its foundation in 1478, the special concern of this particular scuola was the relief of the sick – a continuation of the Christian mission of its patron saint, **St Roch** (Rocco) of Montpellier, who in 1315 left his home town to work among plague victims in Italy. The Scuola had been going for seven years when the body of the saint was brought to Venice from Germany, and the consequent boom in donations was so great that in 1489 it acquired the status of *scuola grande*. In 1527 the city was hit by an outbreak of plague, and the Scuola's revenue rocketed to record levels as gifts poured in from people hoping to secure St Roch's protection against the disease. The fattened coffers paid for this building, and for **Tintoretto**'s amazing cycle of more than fifty major paintings.

The narrative sequence begins with the first picture in the lower room – the *Annunciation*. But to appreciate Tintoretto's development you have to begin in the smaller room on the upper storey – the **Sala dell'Albergo**. This is dominated

### The Scuole

The Venetian institutions known as the **scuole** originated in 1260 with the forma-tion of the confraternity called **Scuola di Santa Maria della Carità**, the first of the so-called **Scuole Grande**. By the middle of the sixteenth century there were five more of these major confraternities – **San Giovanni Evangelista**, **San Marco**, **Santa Maria della Misericordia**, **San Rocco** and **San Teodoro** – plus scores of smaller bodies known as the **Scuole Minore**, of which at one time there were as many as four hundred. The Scuole Grande, drawing much of their membership from the wealthiest professional and mercantile groups, and with rosters of up to six hundred men, received subscriptions that allowed them to fund lavish archi-tectural and artistic projects, of which the Scuola Grande di San Rocco is the most spectacular example. The Scuole Minore, united by membership of certain guilds (eg goldsmiths at the Scuola dei Battioro e Tiraori) or by common nationality (as with San Giorgio degli Schiavoni, the Slavs' scuola), generally operated from far more modest bases. Yet all scuole had the same basic functions – to provide assistance for their members (eg dowries and medical aid), to offer a place of communal worship, and to distribute alms and services in emergencies (anything from plague relief to the provision of troops).

by the stupendous *Crucifixion* (1565), the most compendious image of the event ever painted. Henry James made even greater claims for it: "Surely no single picture in the world contains more of human life; there is everything in it." Tintoretto's other works here – aside from the *Glorification of St Roch* in the middle of the ceiling (the piece that won him the contract to decorate the whole room) – are on the entrance wall.

Tintoretto finished his contribution to the Sala dell'Albergo in 1567. Eight years later, when the Scuola decided to proceed with the embellishment of the main upper hall – the **chapter house** – he undertook to do the work in return for nothing more than his expenses. In the event he was awarded a lifetime annuity, and then commenced the ceiling. The Scuola's governors were so pleased with these three large panels that he was given the task of completing the decoration of the entire interior. The New Testament scenes around the walls defy every convention of perspective, lighting, colour and even anatomy, a feat of sustained inventiveness that has few equals in western art. Though he was in his late sixties when he came to paint the lower hall, there is no sign of flagging creativity: indeed, the landscapes in the *Flight into Egypt* and the meditative depictions of *St Mary Magdalen* and *St Mary of Egypt* are among the finest he ever created.

### The church of San Rocco

Daily 8am–noon & 3–5pm. Yet more Tintorettos are to be found in the neighbouring church of San Rocco. On the right wall of the nave you'll find *St Roch Taken to Prison*, and below it *The Pool of Bethesda*; only the latter is definitely by Tintoretto. Between the altars on the other side are a couple of good pictures by Pordenone – *St Christopher* and *St Martin*. Four large paintings by Tintoretto hang in the chancel, often either lost in the gloom or glazed with sunlight: the best (both painted in 1549) are *St Roch Curing the Plague Victims* (lower right) and *St Roch in Prison* (lower left).

### San Pantaleone

Mon–Sat 4–6pm. The church of San Pantaleone, a short distance to the south of San Rocco, has the most melodramatic ceiling in Venice. Painted on sixty panels, some of which actually jut out over the nave, *The Martyrdom and Apotheosis of St Pantaleone* kept Gian Antonio Fumiani busy from 1680 to 1704. Sadly, he never got the chance to bask in the glory of his labours – he died in a fall from the scaffolding from which he'd been working. In addition, the church possesses a fine picture by Antonio Vivarini and Giovanni d'Alemagna (in the chapel to the left of the chancel) and Veronese's last painting, *St Pantaleone Healing a Boy* (second chapel on right).

### The Scuola di San Giovanni Evangelista

Another of the Scuole Grande nestles in a line of drab buildings very near to the Frari – the Scuola di San Giovanni Evangelista. This institution's finest hour came in 1369, when it was presented with a relic of the True Cross. The miracles effected by the relic were commemorated in a series of paintings by Carpaccio, Gentile

Bellini and others, now transplanted to the Accademia. Nowadays the chief attraction of the Scuola is the superb screen of the outer courtyard, built in 1481 by Pietro Lombardo. Approached from the train station direction, the screen just looks like any old brick wall, but its other face is a wonderfully delicate piece of marble carving.

### The Tolentini and the Giardino Papadopoli

Calle della Lacca–Fondamenta Sacchere–Calle Amai is a dullish but uncomplicated route from San Giovanni Evangelista to the portentous church of San Nicolò da Tolentino – alias the **Tolentini** (daily 8am–noon & 4.30–6.30pm). Among its scores of seventeenth-century paintings, two really stand out: a *St Jerome* by Johann Lys, on the wall outside the chancel, to the left; and *St Lawrence Giving Alms* by Bernardo Strozzi, round the corner from the Lys painting. Up the left wall of the chancel swirls the best Baroque monument in Venice: the **tomb of Francesco Morosini**,

created in 1678 by a Genoese sculptor, Filippo Parodi.

If fatigue is setting in and you need a pit stop, make for the nearby **Giardino Papadopoli**, formerly one of Venice's biggest private gardens but now owned by the city.

## Shops

### Bottega dei Mascareri

Calle del Cristo 2919. Run for many years by the brothers Sergio and Massimo Boldrin, the Bottega dei Mascareri sells some wonderfully inventive masks, such as faces taken from Tiepolo paintings or Donald Sutherland in Fellini's *Casanova*.

### Francis Model

Ruga Rialto 773a. A father-and-son workshop that produces high-quality handbags and briefcases.

### La Scialuppa

Calle Seconda Saoneri. For a uniquely Venetian gift, call in at Gilberto Penzo's shop, which sells well-priced models, model kits and elegantly drawn plans for Venetian boats.

▼ GIARDINO PAPADOPOLI

### Polliero

Campo dei Frari 2995. A bookbinding workshop that sells patterned paper as well as heavy, leather-bound albums of handmade plain paper.

### Rialto market

The market of markets, where you can buy everything you need for an impromptu feast – wine, cheese (the best stalls in the city are here), fruit, salami, vegetables, and bread from nearby bakers or *alimentari* (delicatessens).

### Tragicomica

Calle dei Nomboli 2800. Open daily. A good range of masks and some nice eighteenth-century styles, as you might expect from a shop that's opposite Goldoni's house.

### Valeria Bellinaso

Campo Sant'Aponal 1226. Delicate silk and velvet shoes, bags, hats and gloves.

## Cafés and pasticcerie

### Tonolo

Crosera S. Pantalon 3764. Closed Mon. One of the busiest cafés on one of the busiest streets of the student district; especially hectic on Sunday mornings, when the fancy *Tonolo* cakes are in high demand.

## Restaurants

### Ae Oche

Calle del Tentor 1552. Daily noon–3pm & 7pm–midnight, until 1am Fri & Sat. Excellent rustic pizzeria on an alley that leads into the south

▲ BOTTEGA DEI MASCARERI

side of Campo S. Giacomo dell'Orio. Has about eighty varieties to choose from, so if this doesn't do you, nothing will; on summer evenings if you're not there by 8pm you may have to queue on the pavement.

### Alla Madonna

Calle della Madonna 594. Closed Wed. Roomy, loud and bustling seafood restaurant that's been going strong for four decades. Little finesse but good value for money, and many locals rate its kitchen as one of the city's best, though standards are far from consistent. Reservations not accepted, so be prepared to queue.

### Bancogiro

Sottoportego del Banco Giro 122. Open until midnight, closed Sun evening and all Mon. Popular small brick-vaulted restaurant-cum-bar, in a splendid location by the Rialto market. Come here to sample the innovative, moderately

priced food or just to nurse a glass of fine wine beside the Canal Grande.

### Da Fiore

Calle del Scaleter 2202a
☎041.731.308. Closed Sun & Mon. Refined, elegant restaurant off Campo San Polo; prides itself on its seafood, regional cheeses, desserts, homemade bread and wine list. Generally considered among the very best in Venice, and service is faultless. You can also drop into the tiny front-room bar for a glass of high-quality wine.

### Da Sandro

Campiello dei Meloni. Open until 12.30am, closed Fri. Split-site pizzeria-trattoria, with rooms on both sides of the campiello and tables on the pavement. Often frenetic, though not aggressively so. The pizzas are the best thing they do.

### Il Refolo

Campiello del Piovan 1459. Closed Mon, and Tues lunch. Run by the son of the owner of the famous *Da Fiore*, this excellent canalside pizzeria fills up the tiny square which fronts the church of San Giacomo dell'Orio. Good for salads as well.

### Jazz Club 900

Campiello del Sansoni 900. Open until midnight or later, closed Mon. Just off Ruga Vecchia S. Giovanni, the dark-panelled *Novecento* serves some of the best pizzas in the city, accompanied by non-stop jazz (live on Wednesdays except in summer).

### La Zucca

Ponte del Megio 1762
☎041.524.1570. Closed Sun. Long a well-respected restaurant, *La Zucca* was once a vegetarian establishment (its name means "pumpkin") but now goes against the Venetian grain by featuring a lot of meat – chicken, lamb, beef – and curries. The quality remains high, the prices moderate and the canalside setting is nice.

▲ DO MORI

### Osteria al Ponte, "La Patatina"

2741a Calle dei Saoneri. Closed Sun. Bustling osteria, serving excellent *cicheti* and other Venetian specialities, with well-priced set menus that change regularly.

### Ribò

Fondamenta Minotto 158 ☎041.524.2486. Closed Wed. Co-owned by Matteo Serena, former chef at *Da Fiore*, this is an airy modern establishment (grey marble floors, white walls) where the cuisine is light and modern too. The "business lunch" is something of a bargain at €20, but in the evening expect to pay at least twice that.

## Bars and snacks

### Antico Dolo

Ruga Vecchia S. Giovanni 778. Closed Sun. Excellent *osteria*-style establishment, a good source of wine and snacks near the Rialto.

### Café Blue

Calle dei Preti 3778. Mon–Sat 8am–2am. Lively student haunt where afternoon teas and cakes are on offer as well as whiskies and cocktails. Puts on art exhibitions, has a DJ on Wednesdays, and hosts local rock bands from time to time.

### Café Noir

Crosera San Pantalon 3805. Open Mon–Sat 7am–2am, Sun 7pm–2am. With the neighbouring *Café Blue*, this is candidate for the title of favourite student bar, with a cosmopolitan all-day crowd chatting over a *spritz* or coffee.

### Do Mori

Calle Do Mori 429. Mon–Sat 8.30am–8.30pm. Hidden just off Ruga Vecchia S. Giovanni, this is the most authentic old-style Venetian bar in the market area – some would say in the entire city. It's a single narrow room, with no seating, packed every evening with home-bound shopworkers, Rialto porters, and locals just out for a stroll. Delicious snacks, great range of wines, terrific atmosphere.

# Cannaregio

The hustle around the train station is a misleading
introduction to Cannaregio, because in this sestiere it's
very easy to get well away from the tourist crowds. The
pleasures of Cannaregio are generally more a matter of
atmosphere than of specific sights, but you shouldn't
leave Venice without seeing the **Ghetto**, the first area in
the world to bear that name. There are some special
buildings to visit too: **Madonna dell'Orto**, with its

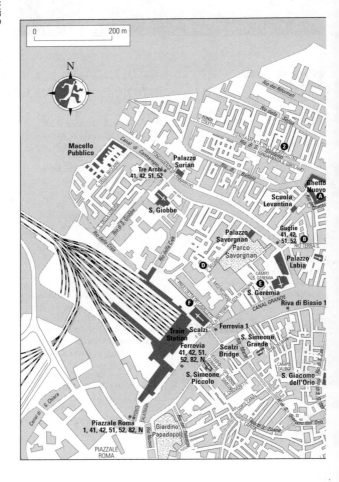

astonishing Tintoretto paintings; **Sant'Alvise** and the **Palazzo Labia**, both remarkable for work by Giambattista Tiepolo; the **Ca' d'Oro**, a gorgeous Canal Grande palace housing a good art collection; and the **Gesuiti**, a Baroque creation which boasts perhaps the weirdest interior in the city.

### The Scalzi

Daily 7–11.50am & 4–6.50pm. Right by the station stands the Scalzi (formally Santa Maria di Nazaretta), which was begun in 1672 for the barefoot ("scalzi") order of Carmelites, but is anything but barefoot itself –

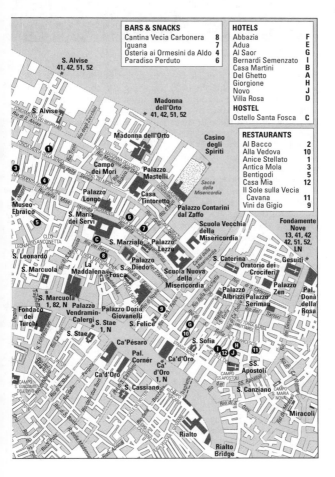

**BARS & SNACKS**

| | |
|---|---|
| Cantina Vecia Carbonera | 8 |
| Iguana | 7 |
| Osteria ai Ormesini da Aldo | 4 |
| Paradiso Perduto | 6 |

**HOTELS**

| | |
|---|---|
| Abbazia | F |
| Adua | E |
| Al Saor | G |
| Bernardi Semenzato | I |
| Casa Martini | B |
| Del Ghetto | A |
| Giorgione | H |
| Novo | J |
| Villa Rosa | D |

**HOSTEL**

| | |
|---|---|
| Ostello Santa Fosca | C |

**RESTAURANTS**

| | |
|---|---|
| Al Bacco | 2 |
| Alla Vedova | 10 |
| Anice Stellato | 1 |
| Antica Mola | 3 |
| Bentigodi | 5 |
| Casa Mia | 12 |
| Il Sole sulla Vecia Cavana | 11 |
| Vini da Gigio | 9 |

▲ PALAZZO LABIA AND SAN GEREMIA

the opulent interior is plated with dark, multicoloured marble and overgrown with Baroque statuary. Before an Austrian bomb plummeted through the roof in 1915 there was a splendid Giambattista Tiepolo ceiling here; a couple of scraps are preserved in the Accademia, and some wan frescoes by Tiepolo survive in the first chapel on the left and the second on the right. The second chapel on the left is the resting place of Lodovico Manin (d.1802), Venice's last doge.

## San Geremia

Mon–Sat 8am–noon & 3.30–6.30pm, Sun 9.15am–12.15pm & 5.30–6.30pm. The church of San Geremia, at the end of the tawdry Lista di Spagna, is where the travels of St Lucy eventually terminated – martyred in Syracuse in 304, she was stolen from Constantinople by Venetian Crusaders in 1204, then ousted from her own church in Venice in the mid-nineteenth century, when it was demolished to make way for the train station. Her dessicated body, wearing a lustrous silver mask, lies behind the altar; nothing else about the church is of interest, except the twelfth-century campanile, one of the oldest left in the city.

## Palazzo Labia

The Palazzo Labia, next door to San Geremia, was built in 1720–50 for a famously extravagant Catalan family by the name of Lasbias. No sooner was the interior completed than Giambattista Tiepolo was hired to cover the walls of the ballroom with frescoes depicting the story of Anthony and Cleopatra. Restored to something approaching its original freshness after years of neglect, this is the only sequence of Tiepolo paintings in Venice that is comparable to his narrative masterpieces in mainland villas such as the Villa Valmarana near Vicenza. RAI, the Italian state broadcasting company, now owns the palace, but they allow visitors in for a few hours each week (usually Wed, Thurs & Fri 3–4pm; free admission is often granted at the door).

## San Giobbe

Mon–Sat 10am–noon & 4–6pm. The Palazzo Labia's longest facade overlooks the Canale di Cannaregio, the main entrance to Venice before the rail and road links were constructed; if you turn left along its fondamenta rather than going with the flow over the Ponte delle Guglie, you'll reach the Ponte dei Tre Archi (Venice's only multiple-span bridge) and the church of San Giobbe. Dedicated to Job, whose sufferings greatly endeared him to the Venetians (who were regularly afflicted with malaria, plague and a plethora of water-related diseases), the church is interesting mainly for its exquisitely carved doorway and chancel – the first Venetian projects of Pietro Lombardo. The tomb with the ludicrous lions is the resting place of the magnificently named Renato de Voyer de Palmy Signore d'Argeson, who served as French ambassador to Venice.

## The Ghetto

The name of the Venetian Ghetto – a name bequeathed to all other such enclaves of oppression – is probably derived from the Venetian dialect *geto*, foundry, which is what this area used to be. The creation of the Ghetto was a consequence of the War of the League of Cambrai, when hundreds of Jews fled the mainland in fear of the Imperial army. Gaining safe haven in Venice, many of the fugitives donated funds for the defence of the city, and were rewarded with permanent protection – at a price. In 1516 the **Ghetto Nuovo** became Venice's Jewish quarter, when all the city's Jews were forced to move onto this small island in the north of Cannaregio. At night the Ghetto was sealed by gates, yet Venice was markedly liberal by the standards of the time, and the Ghetto's population was often swelled by refugees from less tolerant societies – indeed, the Jewish population soon spread into the **Ghetto Vecchio** (1541) and the **Ghetto Nuovissimo** (1633). The gates of the Ghetto were finally torn down by Napoleon in 1797, but it wasn't until the unification of Italy that Jews achieved equal status with their fellow citizens.

Each wave of Jewish immigrants maintained their own synagogues with their distinctive rites: the Scola Tedesca (for German Jews) was founded in 1528, the Scola al Canton (probably Jews from Provence) in 1531–32, the Scola Levantina (eastern Mediterranean) in 1538, the Scola Spagnola (Spanish) at an uncertain date in the later sixteenth century, and the Scola Italiana in 1575. Funded by particularly prosperous trading

▼ THE MUSEO EBRAICO

communities, the Scola Levantina and the Scola Spagnola are the most lavish of the synagogues, and are the only two still used on a daily basis.

Depending on the season, one of the above can be viewed, along with the Scola al Canton and the Scola Italiana, in an informative English-language guided tour that begins in the **Museo Ebraico**, above the Scola Tedesca (daily except Sat & Jewish holidays: June–Sept 10am–7pm; Oct–May 10am–4.30pm; €3 or free with tour, which costs €8; tours in English on the half-hour, last tour 5.30pm in summer, 3.30pm in winter; ⓦwww.jewishvenice.org). The museum's collection consists mainly of silverware, sacred objects, textiles and furniture.

In the northern corner of the campo is a reminder of the ultimate suffering of the Jewish people: a series of seven reliefs by Arbit Blatas commemorating the 200 Venetian Jews deported to the Nazi death camps.

### Sant'Alvise

Mon–Sat 10am–5pm, Sun 1–5pm. €2 or Chorus Pass – see p.171. Located on the northern periphery of the city, the church of Sant'Alvise is notoriously prone to damp, but restoration has refreshed the chancel's immense *Road to Calvary* by Giambattista Tiepolo. His *Crown of Thorns* and *Flagellation*, slightly earlier works, hang on the right-hand wall of the nave. Under the nuns' choir you'll find eight small paintings, known as "The Baby Carpaccios" since Ruskin assigned them to the painter's precocious childhood; they're not actually by Carpaccio, but were produced around 1470, when he would indeed have been just an infant. "Alvise", by the way, is the Venetian version of Louis/Luigi – the church is dedicated to St Louis of Toulouse.

### Campo dei Mori

To get from Sant'Alvise to Madonna dell'Orto you can either take a one-stop vaporetto trip, or cross over the canal to the Fondamenta della Sensa, the main street immediately to the south. Going this way you'll come across the Campo dei Mori, a square whose name may come from the four thirteenth-century statues around the campo. They are popularly associated with a family of merchants called the Mastelli brothers, who used to live in the palace into which two of the figures are embedded – they hailed from the Morea (the Peloponnese), and hence were known as *Mori*. Venice's more malicious citizens used to leave denunciations at the feet of "Sior Antonio Rioba" (the statue with the rusty nose), and circulate vindictive verses signed with his name.

▼ CAMPO DEI MORI

▲ MADONNA DELL'ORTO

## Madonna dell'Orto

Mon–Sat 10am–5pm, Sun 1–5pm. €2
or Chorus Pass – see p.171.
Madonna dell'Orto, the
Tintoretto family's parish
church, is arguably the finest
Gothic church in Venice.
Founded in the name of St
Christopher some time around
1350, it was popularly renamed
after a large stone *Madonna* by
Giovanni de'Santi, found in a
nearby vegetable garden (*orto*),
began working miracles; brought
into the church in 1377, the
heavily restored figure now sits
in the Cappella di San Mauro.

Outside, the church is notable
for its statue of *St Christopher*, its
elegent portal and its campanile,
one of the most notable
landmarks when approaching
Venice from the northern
lagoon. Inside, paintings by
Tintoretto make a massive
impact, none more so than the
epic picures on each side of the
choir: *The Last Judgement* and
*The Making of the Golden Calf.*
Other Tintorettos adorn the

chancel, but none is a match for
the tender *Presentation of the
Virgin*, at the end of the right
aisle, which makes a fascinating
comparison with Titian's
Accademia version of the
incident. A major figure of the
early Venetian Renaissance –
Cima da Conegliano – is
represented by a *St John the
Baptist and Other Saints*, on the
first altar on the right; a
*Madonna and Child* by Cima's
great contemporary, Giovanni
Bellini, used to occupy the first
chapel on the left, but thieves
made off with it in 1993.

## Strada Nova

The main land route between
the train station and the Rialto
bridge was created in the 1870s
by the Austrians. But whereas
the Lista di Spagna and Rio
Terrà San Leonardo were
formed by filling canals with
earth, the Strada Nova was
created by simply ploughing a
line straight through the houses
that used to stand there. Outside

the church of Santa Fosca, at the start of Strada Nova, stands a statue of a true Venetian hero, **Fra' Paolo Sarpi**. A brilliant scholar and scientist (he assisted Galileo's researches), Sarpi was the adviser to the Venetian state in its row with the Vatican at the start of the seventeenth century, when the whole city was excommunicated for its refusal to accept papal jurisdiction in secular affairs. One night Sarpi was walking home past Santa Fosca when he was set upon by three men and left for dead with a dagger in his face. "I recognize the style of the Holy See," Sarpi quipped, punning on the word "stiletto". He survived.

Across the Strada Nova, the **Farmacia Ponci** has the oldest surviving shop interior in Venice, a wonderful display of seventeenth-century heavy-duty woodwork in walnut, kitted out with eighteenth-century majolica vases.

## Ca' d'Oro

Mon 8.15am–2pm, Tues–Sat 8.15am–7.15pm. €5. An inconspicuous calle leads down to the Ca' d'Oro (House of Gold), the showpiece of domestic Gothic architecture in Venice and home of the **Galleria Giorgio Franchetti**. The gallery's main attraction is undoubtedly the *St Sebastian* painted by **Mantegna** shortly before his death in 1506, now installed in a chapel-like alcove on the first floor. Many of the big names of Venetian art are found on the second floor, but the canvases by Titian and Tintoretto are not among their best, and you'll get more out of pieces from less well-known artists – such as Tullio Lombardo's beautifully carved *Young Couple*. Look out too for an anonymous *Madonna and Child* in the midst of the Flemish collection, a sixteenth-century English alabaster polyptych of *Scenes from the Life of St Catherine*, and a case of Renaissance medals containing fine specimens by Gentile Bellini and Pisanello.

▼ CA' D'ORO WELL-HEAD

## Santi Apostoli

Daily 7.30–11.30am & 5–7pm. At the eastern end of the Strada you come to the Campo dei Santi Apostoli, an elbow on the road from the Rialto to the train station. The most interesting part of **Santi Apostoli** church is the **Cappella Corner**, off the right side, where the altarpiece is the *Communion of St Lucy* by Giambattista Tiepolo. One of the inscriptions in the chapel is to Caterina Cornaro, who was buried here before being moved to San Salvatore; the tomb of her father Marco (on the right) is probably by Tullio Lombardo, who also carved the peculiar plaque of St Sebastian in the chapel to the right of the chancel.

111

PLACES Cannaregio

▲ THE GESUITI

## The Gesuiti

Daily 10am–noon & 4–6pm. The
major monument in the
northeastern corner of
Cannaregio is Santa Maria
Assunta, commonly known
simply as the Gesuiti. Built for
the Jesuits in 1714–29, six
decades after the foundation
here of their first monastery in
Venice, the church was clearly
planned to make an impression
on a city that was habitually
mistrustful of the order's close
relationship with the papacy.
Although the disproportionately
huge facade clearly wasn't the
work of a weekend, most of the
effort went into the stupefying
interior, where green and white
marble covers every wall and
stone is carved to resemble
swags of damask. The only
painting to seek out is the
*Martyrdom of St Lawrence* on the
first altar on the left, which was
painted by **Titian** in 1558.

## The Fondamente Nove

The long waterfront to the
north of the Gesuiti, the
Fondamente Nove (or Nuove),
is the point at which the
vaporetti leave the city for San
Michele, Murano and the
northern lagoon. On a clear day
you can follow their course as
far as the distant island of
Burano, and you might even be
treated to the startling sight of
the snowy Dolomite peaks,
apparently hanging in the sky
over the Veneto.

# Restaurants

## Al Bacco

Fondamenta delle Cappuccine 3054
☎041.717.493. Closed Mon. Like the
*Antica Mola*, further east along
the canal, *Al Bacco* started life as
a humble neighbourhood stop-
off, but has grown into a fully
fledged restaurant, with prices to
match. It retains a rough-and-
ready feel, but the food is
distinctly classy.

## Alla Vedova

Calle del Pistor 3912. Closed all Thurs
& Sun lunch. Located in an alley
directly opposite the one
leading to the Ca' d'Oro, this
long-established and modestly
priced little restaurant is fronted
by a bar offering a
mouthwatering selection of

*cicheti* (the *polpette* are famous) and a good range of wines. No credit cards.

### Anice Stellato

Fondamenta della Sensa 3272 ☎041.720.744. Closed Mon & Tues. Hugely popular with Venetians for the superb, reasonably priced meals and unfussy atmosphere. Situated by one of the northernmost Cannaregio canals, it's rather too remote for most tourists. If you can't get a table – it's frequently booked solid – at least drop by for the excellent *cicheti* at the bar.

### Antica Mola

Fondamenta degli Ormesini 2800. Closed Wed. This family-run trattoria, near the Ghetto, has become very popular with tourists, but the food remains good value. There's a nice garden at the back and canalside tables out front.

### Bentigodi

Calle Sele 1423 ☎041.716.269. Closed Sun & Mon. Friendly modern *osteria* just outside the ghetto, run by Elena, whose husband runs *Bancogiro* in San Polo. She serves the same inventive and moderately priced Venetian dishes, backed up by an extensive wine list. No credit cards. Booking advisable.

### Casa Mia

Calle dell'Oca 4430. Closed Tues. Always heaving with locals, who usually go for the pizza list rather than the menu, though the standard dishes are reliable enough.

### La Colombina

Campiello del Pegolotto 1828 ☎041.275.0622. Daily 6.30pm–2am. This trendy bar-cum-restaurant has been putting more emphasis

on the lattter aspect of the business recently, with great success. The huge wine list is still crucial to its appeal, but the menu is strikingly dissimilar to many of its mid-range rivals, mixing Venetian aquatic standards with Tuscan meat dishes.

### Il Sole sulla Vecia Cavana

Rio Terá SS Apostoli 4624 ☎041.528.7106, ◉www .veciacavana.it. Closed Mon. The orange walls and wooden panelling create an inviting interior, and the mouth-watering menu, carefully assembled by owner Stefano Monti, is similarly appealing, ranging from a wonderful tuna tartare to a deliciously strange basil ice-cream. Not cheap, but well worth the money. Excellent wines.

### Vini da Gigio

Fondamenta S. Felice 3628a. Closed Mon. Popular, family-run wine bar-trattoria. It's now on the tourist map yet it retains its authenticity and is still, by Venetian standards, excellent value.

# Bars and snacks

### Cantina Vecia Carbonera

Rio Terrà della Maddalena 2329. Open till 11pm most nights, closed Mon. Old-style *bacarò* atmosphere and chilled-out playlist attract a young, stylish clientele. Good wine, excellent snacks and plenty of space to sit down.

### Iguana

Fondamenta della Misericordia 2517. Open Tues–Sun till 2am, happy hour 6–7.30pm. This cross between a *bacarò* and a Mexican cantina serves reasonably priced Tex-Mex fare to a young crowd.

Live music (Latin, rock and jazz) Tues 9–11pm.

### Osteria ai Ormesini da Aldo

Fondamenta degli Ormesini 2710. Open Mon–Sat till 2am. One of a number of bars beside this long canal, and a particularly pleasant spot for a lunchtime snack in the sun.

### Paradiso Perduto

Fondamenta della Misericordia 2540. Open 7.30pm to midnight or later, closed Wed. Lashings of simple (but not always inexpensive) Venetian food are served at refectory-like tables, but essentially this place is Venice's leading boho bar, attracting students, arty types and the gay community. Music – blues, jazz or whatever – usually on Sun, sometimes Mon.

▲ CANTINA VECIA CARBONERA

PLACES  Cannaregio

# Central Castello

Bordering San Marco on one side and spreading across the city from Cannaregio in the west to the housing estates of Sant'Elena in the east, Castello is so unwieldy a sestiere that somewhat altered boundaries have been used in laying out our guide. In the west, this chapter starts off from the waterway that cuts round the back of Santi Apostoli to the northern lagoon, and stops in the east at a line drawn north from the landmark Pietà church; the atmospherically distinct area beyond this boundary is covered in the next chapter.

The points of interest in this area are evenly distributed, but in terms of its importance and its geographical location, Castello's central building is the immense Gothic church of **Santi Giovanni e Paolo** (or **Zanipolo**), the pantheon of Venice's doges. A couple of minutes away stands the much-loved **Santa Maria dei Miracoli**, which in turn is close to the often overlooked **San Giovanni Crisostomo**. The museums lie in the southern zone – the **Querini-Stampalia** picture collection, the museum at **San Giorgio dei Greci**, and the **Museo Diocesano**'s sacred art collection. This southern area's dominant building is the majestic **San Zaccaria**, right by the southern waterfront and Venice's main promenade, the **Riva degli Schiavoni**.

## San Giovanni Crisostomo

Mon–Sat 8.15am–12.15pm & 3–7pm, Sun 3–7pm. On the western edge of Castello stands San Giovanni Crisostomo (John the Golden-Mouthed), named after the eloquent Archbishop of Constantinople. It was possibly the last project of Mauro Codussi, and possesses two outstanding altarpieces: in the chapel to the right hangs one of the last works by Giovanni Bellini, SS. *Jerome, Christopher and Louis of Toulouse*, painted in 1513 when the artist was in his eighties; and on the high altar, Sebastiano del Piombo's gracefully heavy *St John Chrysostom with SS. John the*

*Baptist, Liberale, Mary Magdalen, Agnes and Catherine*, painted in 1509–11.

## Teatro Malibran

Behind San Giovanni Crisostomo is the Teatro Malibran, which opened in the seventeenth century, was rebuilt in the 1790s, and soon after renamed in honour of the great soprano Maria Malibran (1808–36), who saved the theatre from bankruptcy by giving a fund-raising recital here. Quite recently unveiled following a very protracted restoration, the Malibran is one of the city's chief venues for classical music. The Byzantine

**HOTELS**
| | |
|---|---|
| Al Leon | H |
| Canada | B |
| Caneva | E |
| Casa Querini | G |
| Casa Verardo | F |
| Danieli | K |
| Doni | I |
| Locanda Leon Bianco | A |
| Paganelli | J |
| Scandinavia | D |

**HOSTELS**
| | |
|---|---|
| Foresteria Valdese | C |

**RESTAURANTS**
| | |
|---|---|
| Aciugheta | 12 |
| Alle Testiere | 10 |
| Da Remigio | 11 |
| Fiaschetteria Toscana | 2 |

**CAFÉS & PASTICCERIE**
| | |
|---|---|
| Didovich | 4 |
| La Boutique del Gelato | 8 |
| Rosa Salva | 3 |
| Snack & Sweet | 7 |

**BARS & SNACKS**
| | |
|---|---|
| Al Ponte | 1 |
| Cip Ciap | 9 |
| Enoteca Mascareta | 6 |
| L'Olandese Volante | 5 |
| Osteria da Baco | 13 |

**SHOPS**
| | |
|---|---|
| Filippi Editore Venezia | a & b |
| Kerer | c |

arches on the facade of the theatre are said to have once been part of the house of Marco Polo's family, who probably lived in the heavily restored palace overlooking the canal at the back of the Malibran, visible from the Ponte Marco Polo.

## Santa Maria dei Miracoli

Mon–Sat 10am–5pm, Sun 1–5pm. €2 or Chorus Pass – see p.171. A hop north of here stands the marble-clad church of Santa Maria dei Miracoli, usually known simply by the last word of its name. It was built in 1481–89 to house an image of the Madonna that

▲ SANTA MARIA DEI MIRACOLI

tending the sick and the poor) required a lot of space for their congregrations. The first church built on this site was begun in 1246 after Doge Giacomo Tiepolo was inspired by a dream to donate the land to the Dominicans. Tiepolo's simple sarcophagus is outside, on the left of the door, next to that of his son Doge Lorenzo Tiepolo (d.1275); the cavernous interior – approximately 90 metres long, 38 metres wide at the transepts, 33 metres high in the centre – houses the tombs of some twenty-five other doges.

The finest funerary monuments are in the **chancel**, where Doge Michele Morosini, who ruled for just four months before dying of plague in 1382, is buried in the tomb at the front on the right, a work which to Ruskin's eyes showed "the exactly intermediate condition of feeling between the pure calmness of early Christianity, and the boastful pomp of the Renaissance faithlessness". Full-blown Renaissance pomp is represented by the tomb of Doge Andrea Vendramin (d.1478), diagonally opposite, while one of the earliest examples of Renaissance style in Venice – Pietro Lombardo's tomb for Doge Pasquale Malipiero (d.1462) – is to be found in the left aisle, to the left of the door to the sacristy. (The sacristy itself contains an excellent painting, Alvise Vivarini's *Christ Carrying the Cross*.) The Lombardo family were also responsible for the tombs of Doge Giovanni

was credited with the revival of a man who'd spent half an hour at the bottom of the Giudecca canal and of a woman left for dead after being stabbed. Financed by gifts left at the painting's nearby shrine, the church was most likely designed by Pietro Lombardo; certainly he and his two sons Tullio and Antonio oversaw the construction, and the three of them executed much of the exquisite carving both inside and out. The miracle-working *Madonna* still occupies the altar.

### Santi Giovanni e Paolo

Mon–Sat 7.30am–12.30pm & 3.30–7pm, Sun 3–6pm. Like the Frari, the massive Gothic brick edifice of Santi Giovanni e Paolo – slurred by the Venetian dialect into **San Zanipolo** – was built for one of the mendicant orders, whose social mission (preaching to and

▲ SANTI GIOVANNI E PAOLO

Mocenigo and Doge Pietro
Mocenigo, to the right and left
of the main door. Close by, the
second altar of the right aisle is
adorned by one of Zanipolo's
finest paintings, **Giovanni
Bellini**'s polyptych of *SS.
Vincent Ferrer, Christopher and
Sebastian.*

At the top of the right aisle, *St
Dominic in Glory*, the only
ceiling panel in Venice by
Giambattista Piazzetta,
Giambattista Tiepolo's tutor,
covers the vault of the
**Cappella di San Domenico**,
alongside which is a tiny shrine
containing a relic of St
Catherine of Siena. She died in
1380 and her body promptly
entered the relic market – most
of it is in Rome, but her head is
in Siena, one foot is here, and
other, lesser relics are scattered
about Italy. Round the corner,
in the south transept, two other
superb paintings hang close
together: a *Coronation of the
Virgin* attributed to Cima da
Conegliano and Giovanni
Martini da Udine, and Lorenzo
Lotto's *St Antonine* (1542).

And don't miss the **Cappella
del Rosario**, at the end of the
north transept. In 1867 a fire
destroyed its paintings by
Tintoretto, plus Giovanni
Bellini's *Madonna* and Titian's
*Martyrdom of St Peter*, San
Zanipolo's two most celebrated
paintings. A lengthy twentieth-
century restoration made use of
surviving fragments and installed
other pieces such as Veronese's
ceiling panels of *The
Annunciation, The Assumption* and
*The Adoration of the Shepherds*,
and another *Adoration* by him
on the left of the door.

## The Colleoni monument

When he died in 1475, the
mercenary captain Bartolomeo
Colleoni left a legacy of some
700,000 ducats to the Venetian
state. But there was a snag: the
Signoria could have the money
only if an equestrian monument
to him were erected in the
square before San Marco – an
unthinkable proposition to
Venice's rulers, with their cult of
anonymity. The problem was
circumvented with a fine piece

of disingenuousness, by which Colleoni's will was taken to permit the raising of the statue before the Scuola di San Marco, rather than the Basilica. Andrea Verrocchio's statue wasn't finally unveiled until 1496, but the wait was certainly worth it: this idealized image of steely masculinity is one of the masterpieces of Renaissance sculpture.

### The Scuola Grande di San Marco

Colleoni's backdrop, the Scuola Grande di San Marco, now provides a sumptuous facade and foyer for Venice's hospital. The facade was started by Pietro Lombardo and Giovanni Buora in 1487, half a century after the scuola moved here from its original home over in the Santa Croce sestiere, and finished in 1495 by Mauro Codussi. Taken as a whole, the perspectival panels by Tullio and Antonio Lombardo might not quite create the intended illusion, but they are nonetheless among the most charming sculptural pieces in Venice.

### The Ospedaletto

April–Sept Thurs–Sat 3.30–6.30pm; Oct–March same days 3–6pm.
Another hospital block is attached to the church of the Ospedaletto (or Santa Maria dei Derelitti), beyond the east end of Zanipolo. The leering giants' heads and over-ripe decorations of its facade made it "the most monstrous" building in the city, according to Ruskin. The much less extravagant interior has a series of eighteenth-century paintings high on the walls above the arches, one of which – *The Sacrifice of Isaac* – is an early Giambattista Tiepolo (fourth on the right). The

adjoining music room (€2), frescoed in the eighteenth century, is still used for **concerts**, many of them free.

### Santa Maria Formosa

The wide **Campo di Santa Maria Formosa**, virtually equidistant from the Piazza, San Zanipolo and the Ponte di Rialto, is a major confluence of routes on the east side of the Canal Grande, and one of the most attractive and atmospheric squares in the city.

The **church of Santa Maria Formosa** (Mon–Sat 10am–5pm, Sun 1–5pm; €2, or Chorus Pass – see p.171) was founded in the seventh century by San Magno, Bishop of Oderzo, who was guided by a dream in which he saw the Madonna *formosa* – a word which most closely translates as buxom and beautiful. Outside,

▼CAMPANILE OF SANTA MARIA FORMOSA

the most unusual feature is the mask at the base of the campanile: both a talisman against the evil eye and a depiction of a man with the same rare congenital disorder as disfigured the so-called Elephant Man. The church contains two good paintings. Entering from the west side, the first one you'll see is Bartolomeo Vivarini's triptych of *The Madonna of the Misericordia* (1473), in a nave chapel on the right-hand side of the church. Nearby, closer to the main altar, is Palma il Vecchio's *St Barbara* (1522–24), praised by George Eliot as "an almost unique presentation of a hero-woman". Barbara is the patron saint of artillery-men, which is why the painting shows her treading on a cannon.

### Santa Maria della Fava

Daily 8.30am–noon & 4.30–7.30pm. Between Santa Maria Formosa and the Rialto stands the church of Santa Maria della Fava (or Santa Maria della Consolazione), whose peculiar name derives from a sweet cake called a *fava* (bean), once an All Souls' Day speciality of a local baker and still a seasonal treat. On the first altar on the right stands Giambattista Tiepolo's early *Education of the Virgin* (1732); on the other side of the church there's *The Madonna and St Philip Neri*, painted five years earlier by Giambattista Piazzetta.

### The Querini-Stampalia

Tues–Sun 10am–6pm, until 10pm Fri & Sat. €6. On the south side of Campo Santa Maria Formosa, a footbridge over a narrow canal leads into the Palazzo Querini-Stampalia, home of the **Pinacoteca Querini-Stampalia**. Although there is a batch of Renaissance pieces

here, the general tone is set by the culture of eighteenth-century Venice, a period to which much of the palace's decor belongs. The winningly inept pieces by Gabriel Bella form a comprehensive record of Venetian social life in that century, and the more accomplished genre paintings of Pietro and Alessandro Longhi feature prominently as well. Make sure you take a look at the gardens and ground-floor exhibition space – they were redesigned in the 1960s by the sleek modernist Carlo Scarpa.

### The Museo Diocesano

Daily 10.30am–12.30pm. Donation requested. Beside the Rio di Palazzo, at the back of the Palazzo Ducale, stands the early fourteenth-century cloister of **Sant'Apollonia**, the only Romanesque cloister in the city. Fragments from the Basilica di San Marco dating back to the ninth century are displayed here, and a miscellany of sculptural pieces from other churches are on show in the adjoining **Museo Diocesano d'Arte Sacra**, where the permanent collection consists chiefly of a range of religious artefacts and paintings gathered from churches that have closed down or entrusted their possessions to the safety of the museum. In addition, freshly restored works from other collections or churches sometimes pass through here, giving the museum an edge of unpredictability.

### San Zaccaria

Daily 10am–noon & 4–6pm. East of Sant'Apollonia, the Salizzada di San Provolo, leading east out of Campo Santi Filippo e Giacomo, runs straight to the elegant **Campo San Zaccaria**, a spot with a chequered past. In 864 Doge Pietro Tradonico was murdered in the campo as he returned from vespers, and in 1172 Doge Vitale Michiel II, having not only blundered in peace negotiations with the Byzantine empire but also brought the plague back with him from Constantinople, was murdered as he fled for the sanctuary of San Zaccaria.

Founded in the ninth century as a shrine for the body of Zaccharias, father of John the Baptist, the **church of San Zaccaria** had already been rebuilt several times when, in 1444, Antonio Gambello embarked on a massive rebuilding project that was concluded some seventy years later by Mauro Codussi, who took over the facade from the first storey upwards. The end result is a distinctively Venetian mixture of Gothic and Renaissance styles.

The interior's notable architectural feature is its ambulatory: unique in Venice, it might have been built to accommodate the annual ritual of the doges' Easter Sunday visit. Nearly every inch of wall surface is hung with seventeenth- and eighteenth-century paintings, all of them outshone by Giovanni **Bellini**'s large *Madonna and Four Saints* (1505), on the second altar on the left. The €1 fee payable to enter the Cappella di Sant'Atanasio and Cappella di San Tarasio (off the right aisle) is well worth it for the three wonderful composite altarpieces by Antonio Vivarini and Giovanni d'Alemagna (all 1443). Downstairs is the spooky and perpetually waterlogged ninth-century crypt, the burial place of eight early doges.

## The Riva degli Schiavoni

The broad Riva degli Schiavoni, stretching from the edge of the Palazzo Ducale to the canal just before the Arsenale entrance, is constantly thronged during the day, with

▼ BELLINI'S SAN ZACCARIA ALTARPIECE

an unceasing flow of promenading tourists and passengers hurrying to and from its vaporetto stops, threading through the souvenir stalls and past the wares of the African street vendors. The Riva has long been one of Venice's smart addresses. Petrarch and his daughter lived at no. 4145 in 1362–67, and Henry James stayed at no. 4161, battling against constant distractions to finish *The Portrait of a Lady*. George Sand, Charles Dickens, Proust, Wagner and the ever-present Ruskin all checked in at the *Hotel Danieli* (see p.161).

## The Pietà

Daily 10am–noon & 4–6pm. The main eyecatcher on the Riva is the white facade of Santa Maria della Visitazione, known less cumbersomely as La Pietà. **Vivaldi** wrote many of his finest pieces for the orphanage attached to the church, where he worked as violinmaster (1704–18) and later as choirmaster (1735–38). During Vivaldi's second term Giorgio Massari won a competition to rebuild the church, and it's probable that the composer advised him on acoustics, though building didn't begin until after Vivaldi's death. The white and gold interior is crowned by a superb ceiling painting of *The Glory of Paradise* by Giambattista Tiepolo. Unfortunately the Pietà is still one of Venice's busiest music venues, mostly for second-rate renditions of Vivaldi favourites, and just about the only time you can get a peek inside is when the box office is open.

## The Greek quarter

A couple of minutes' walk north of La Pietà, the campanile of **San Giorgio dei Greci** (Mon–Sat 9.30am–1pm & 3.30–5.30pm, Sun 9am–1pm) lurches spectacularly canalwards. The Greek presence in Venice was strong from the eleventh century, and became stronger still after the Turkish seizure of Constantinople. Built a century later, the church has Orthodox architectural elements including a *matroneo* (women's gallery) above the main entrance and an iconostasis (or rood screen) that completely cuts off the high altar. The icons on the screen include a few Byzantine pieces dating back as far as the twelfth century.

The Scuola di San Nicolò dei Greci, to the left of the church, now houses the **Museo di Dipinti Sacri Bizantini** (Mon–Sat 9am–12.30pm & 2–4.30pm, Sun 10am–5pm; €4), a collection of predominantly fifteenth- to eighteenth-century icons, many of them by the *Madoneri*, the school of Greek and Cretan artists working in Venice in that period.

# Shops

## Coin

Salizzada San Giovanni Crisotomo 5790. Founded in Venice, Coin is now a nationwide department store, specialising in clothes. An inexpensive way to acquire a semblance of Italian style.

## Filippi Editore Venezia

Caselleria 5284 & Calle del Paradiso 5763. The family-run Filippi business produces a vast range of Venice-related facsimile editions, including Francesco Sansovino's sixteenth-century guide to the city (the first city guide ever published) and sells

▲ FILIPPI EDITORE VENEZIA

an amazing stock of books about Venice in its two shops.

### Kerer

Palazzo Trevisan-Cappello, on Rio Canonica. Occupying part of a huge palazzo at the rear of the Basilica di San Marco, this vast showroom sells a wide range of lace, both affordable and exclusive.

# Cafés and pasticcerie

### Didovich

Campo Marina 5910. Open Mon–Sat till 8pm. A new but already highly regarded *pasticceria* – some say with the city's best tiramisù and *pastine* (aubergine, pumpkin and other savoury tarts). Standing room only inside, but has outdoor tables.

### La Boutique del Gelato

Salizzada S. Lio 5727. Open daily. Top-grade ice creams at this small outlet.

### Rosa Salva

Campo Santi Giovanni e Paolo. Another branch of Venice's leading café chain. Excellent coffee, if low on charisma.

### Snack & Sweet

Salizzada S. Lio 5689. Closed Sat. *Pasticceria* and bar with a glorious spread of cakes and sandwiches.

# Restaurants

### Aciugheta

Campo SS. Filippo e Giacomo 4357. Closed Wed. A bar with a sizeable pizzeria-trattoria attached. The closest spot to San Marco to eat without paying through the nose, it draws a lot of its custom from waterbus staff and gondoliers. Good bar food to nibble or have as a meal. The name translates as "the little anchovy" and there are paintings of anchovies on the wall.

### Alle Testiere

Calle Mondo Nuovo 5801 ☎041.522.7220. Closed Sun & Mon,

▼ ACIUGHETA

and mid-July to mid-Aug. Very small mid-range seafood restaurant near Santa Maria Formosa, with excellent daily specials and a superb wine selection. Sittings at 7pm and 9pm to handle the demand.

## Da Remigio

Salizzada dei Greci 3416 ☎041.523.0089. Closed Mon evening and all Tues. Brilliant trattoria, serving gorgeous homemade *gnocchi*. Be sure to book – the locals pack this place every night. Prices are rising in tandem with its burgeoning reputation, but are still reasonable.

## Fiaschetteria Toscana

Salizzada S. Giovanni Crisostomo 5719 ☎041.528.5281. Closed Mon lunch, Tues, a few days after Carnevale and mid-July to mid-Aug. The name of this upmarket restaurant means "Tuscan Wine Shop", but the menu is quintessentially Venetian. Highly rated for its food, the Fiaschetteria also has an excellent wine list. The service is immaculate, and the place has an understated elegance.

# Bars and snacks

## Al Ponte

Calle Larga G. Gallina 6378. Open till 8.30pm, closed Sun. Typical *osteria* just off Campo Santi Giovanni e Paolo. Good for a glass of wine and a snack.

## Cip Ciap

Calle Mondo Nuovo 5799. Open 9am–9pm, closed Tues. Located across the canal from the west side of Santa Maria Formosa, this place offers the widest range of take-out pizza slices (*pizza al taglio*) in the city.

## Enoteca Mascareta

Calle Lunga Santa Maria Formosa 5183. Mon–Sat 6pm–1am. Buzzing wine bar with delicious snacks.

## L'Olandese Volante

Campo San Lio. Open until 12.30am, until 2am Fri & Sat, closed Sun morning. The "Flying Dutchman" is a busy brasserie-style pub with plenty of outdoor tables.

## Osteria da Baco

Calle delle Rasse 4620. Open daily until midnight or later. Traditional-style *osteria*, with a wide selection of filling sandwiches.

# Music

## Teatro Malibran

Corte Milion 5873. The city's main venue for big-name classical concerts, but it also hosts the occasional major-league jazz gig and Italian rockers such as Ligabue. Tickets usually start at around €30 (with discounts for under-30s), and can be bought in advance from the Fenice box office (see p.75) or the Cassa di Risparmio di Venezia, Campo San Luca (see p.66). The Malibran ticket office sells tickets only on the night of the concert, from around 30min before the start.

# Eastern Castello

For all that most visitors see of the eastern section of the Castello sestiere, the city may as well peter out a few metres beyond the Palazzo Ducale. Sights are thinly spread here, and a huge bite is taken out of the area by the wharves of the Arsenale, yet the slab of the city immediately to the west of the Arsenale contains places

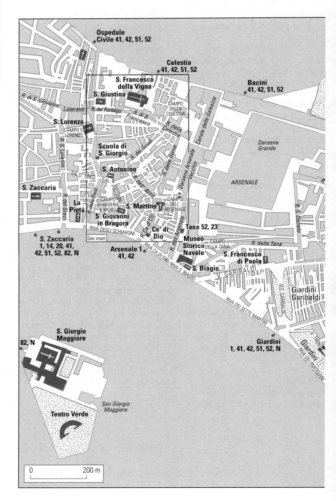

that shouldn't be ignored – the Renaissance **San Francesco della Vigna**, for example, and the **Scuola di San Giorgio degli Schiavoni**, with its endearing cycle of paintings by **Carpaccio**. And although the mainly residential area beyond the Arsenale has little to offer in the way of cultural monuments other than the ex-cathedral of **San Pietro di Castello** and the church of **Sant'Elena**, it would be a mistake to leave the easternmost zone unexplored. For one thing, the whole

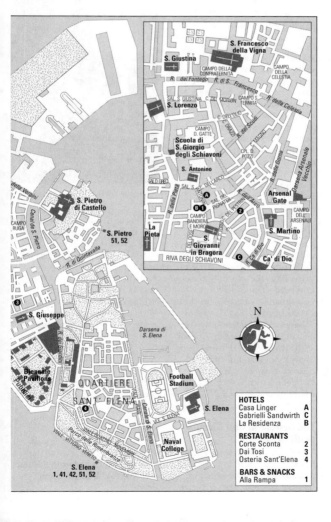

| HOTELS | |
| --- | --- |
| Casa Linger | A |
| Gabrielli Sandwirth | C |
| La Residenza | B |
| **RESTAURANTS** | |
| Corte Sconta | 2 |
| Dai Tosi | 3 |
| Osteria Sant'Elena | 4 |
| **BARS & SNACKS** | |
| Alla Rampa | 1 |

length of the waterfront gives spectacular panoramas of the city, with the best coming last.

## San Francesco della Vigna

Daily 8am–12.30pm & 3–6.30pm. The area that lies to the east of San Zanipolo is not an attractive district at first sight, but carry on east for just a couple of minutes and a striking Renaissance facade blocks your way. The ground occupied by San Francesco della Vigna has a hallowed place in the mythology of Venice, as according to tradition it was around here that the angel appeared to St Mark to tell him that the lagoon islands were to be his final resting place. Begun in 1534, the present building was much modified in the course of its construction. Palladio was brought in to provide the facade, a feature that looks like something of an afterthought from the side, but which must have been stunning at the time.

The interior has some fine works of art, notably a glowingly colourful *Madonna and Child Enthroned* by Antonio da Negroponte (right transept), marvellous sculpture by the Lombardo family in the Giustiniani chapel (left of the chancel), and a *Sacra Conversazione* by Veronese (last chapel of the left aisle). A door at the end of the transept leads to a pair of tranquil fifteenth-century cloisters, via the Cappella Santa, which has a *Madonna and Child* by Giovanni Bellini and assistants.

## The Scuola di San Giorgio degli Schiavoni

April–Oct Tues–Sat 9.30am–12.30pm & 3.30–6.30pm, Sun 9.30am–12.30pm; Nov–March Tues–Sat 10am–12.30pm & 3–6pm,

▲ SAN FRANCESCO DELLA VIGNA

Sun 10am–12.30pm. €3. Venice has two brilliant cycles of pictures by **Vittore Carpaccio**, the most disarming of Venetian artists – one is in the Accademia, the other in the Scuola di San Giorgio degli Schiavoni, the confraternity of Venice's Slavic community. The cycle illustrates mainly the lives of the Dalmatian patron saints – George, Tryphone and Jerome. As always with Carpaccio, what holds your attention is not so much the main event as the incidental details with which he packs the scene, such as the limb-strewn feeding-ground of St George's dragon, or the endearing little white dog in *The Vision of St Augustine* (he was writing to St Jerome when a vision told him of Jerome's death).

### San Giovanni in Brágora

Mon–Sat 9–11am & 3.30–5.30pm.
San Giovanni in Brágora is
probably best known to
Venetians as the baptismal
church of Antonio Vivaldi. The
church is dedicated to the
Baptist, and some people think
that its strange suffix is a
reference to a region from
which some relics of the saint
were once brought; others link
the name to the old dialect
words for mud (*brago*) and
backwater (*gora*). The present
structure was begun in 1475,
and its best paintings were
created within a quarter-century
of the rebuilding: a triptych by
Bartolomeo Vivarini, on the wall
between the first and second
chapels on the right; a
*Resurrection* by Alvise Vivarini, to
the left of the sacristy door; and
two paintings by Cima da
Conegliano – a *SS. Helen and
Constantine*, to the right of the
sacristy door, and a *Baptism* on
the high altar.

### The Arsenale

A corruption of the Arabic
*darsin'a* (house of industry), the
very name of the Arsenale is
indicative of the strength of
Venice's links with the eastern
Mediterranean, and the workers
of these dockyards and factories
were the foundations upon
which the city's maritime
supremacy rested. By the 1420s
it had become the base for some
300 shipping companies,
operating around 3000 vessels of
200 tons or more; at the
Arsenale's zenith, around the
middle of the sixteenth century,
its wet and dry docks, its rope
and sail factories, its ordnance
depots and gunpowder mills
employed a total of 16,000 men
– equal to the population of a
major town of the period.

There is no public access to
the Arsenale, but you can
inspect the magnificent
**gateway** at close quarters. The
first structure in Venice to
employ the classical vocabulary
of Renaissance architecture, it is
guarded by four photogenic
lions brought here from Greece:
the two furthest on the right
probably came from the Lion
Terrace at Delos, and date from
around the sixth century BC;
the larger pair were stolen from
Piraeus in 1687 by Francesco
Morosini.

▼ ARSENALE GATE

▲ MODEL IN THE MUSEO STORICO NAVALE

### The Museo Storico Navale

Mon–Fri 8.45am–1.30pm, Sat 8.45am–1pm. €1.55. Documenting every conceivable facet of Venice's naval history, the Museo Storico Navale is a somewhat diffuse museum, but a selective tour is an essential supplement to a walk round the Arsenale district. Improbable though it sounds, the models of Venetian craft – from the gondola to the 224-oar fighting galley and the last *Bucintoro* (the state ceremonial galley) – will justify the entrance fee for most people.

### Via Garibaldi and San Pietro di Castello

In 1808 the greater part of the canal connecting the Bacino di San Marco to the broad northeastern inlet of the Canale di San Pietro was filled in to form what is now Via Garibaldi, the widest street in the city and the social hub of the eastern district. Via Garibaldi points the way to the island of San Pietro, one of the first parts of central Venice to be inhabited. Nowadays this is a workaday district where the repairing of

boats is the main occupation, yet it was once the ecclesiastical centre of Venice, having been the seat of the Patriarch of Venice until 1807. As with the Arsenale, the history of San Pietro is somewhat more interesting than what you can see. The present **San Pietro di Castello** (Mon–Sat 10am–5pm, Sun 1–5pm; €2 or Chorus Pass – see p.171) is an uncharismatic church, its most engaging features being the so-called Throne of St Peter (right aisle), a marble seat made in the thirteenth century from an Arabic funeral stone cut with texts from the Koran, and the campanile, one of the most precarious in the city.

### The public gardens and the Biennale site

Stretching from Via Garibaldi to the Rio di Sant'Elena, the arc of green spaces formed by the **Giardini Garibaldi**, **Giardini Pubblici** and **Parco delle Rimembranze** provide a remedy for the claustrophobia that overtakes most visitors to Venice at some point. Largely obscured by the trees are the rather more extensive grounds belonging to the **Biennale**, a dormant zone except when the art and architecture shindigs are in progress (in the summer of odd- and even-numbered years respectively). Various countries have built permanent pavilions for their Biennale representatives, forming a unique colony that features work by some of the great names of modern architecture and design, such as Alvar Aalto, Gerrit Thomas Rietveld and Carlo Scarpa.

### Sant'Elena

Mon–Sat 5–7pm. The island of Sant'Elena, the city's eastern limit, was greatly enlarged during the Austrian administration, partly to furnish accommodation and exercise grounds for the occupying troops. Its sole monument is Sant'Elena church, founded in the thirteenth century to house the body of St Helena, Constantine's mother. Approached between the walls of the naval college and the ramshackle home of Venice's second-division football team, it's worth visiting for the fine doorway, an ensemble incorporating the monument to Vittore Cappello, captain-general of the Republic's navy in the 1460s, showing him kneeling before Saint Helena.

▲ SANT'ELENA

*degustazione*, costing €50 (without wine), gives you a chance to sample all their specialities in one gourmet experience, and is probably the best meal that sum will get you in the entire city. If expenditure

# Restaurants

### Corte Sconta

Calle del Pestrin 3886
☎041.522.7024. Closed Sun & Mon.
Secreted in a lane to the east of San Giovanni in Brágora, this restaurant is a candidate for the title of Venice's finest. The *menù*

▼ CORTE SCONTA

is an issue, check the menu in the window carefully before going in (often the waiters will simply recite what's on offer rather than give you anything printed). Booking several days in advance is essential for most of the year.

### Dai Tosi

Calle Secco Marina 738 ☎041.523.7102. Open till 11.30pm, closed Wed, and the kitchen often closes Mon, Tues and/or Thurs in winter. Lively pizzeria-trattoria with a devoted clientele – you'd be well advised to book at the weekend. There's a bar in front of the small dining room, where they mix the house aperitif: *sgropino*, a delicious mingling of vodka, peach juice, Aperol and prosecco. Not to be confused with the establishment of the same name in the same street. Inexpensive to moderate.

### Osteria Sant'Elena

Calle Chinotto 24 ☎041.520.8419. Open till midnight, closed Tues. This utterly genuine neighbourhood restaurant is the preserve of the residents of Sant'Elena except when the Biennale is in full swing. The menu is simple, the cooking good, prices fair, and there's a bar serving *cicheti* at the front; outside tables add to the appeal.

## Bars and snacks

### Alla Rampa

Salizzada S. Antonin 3607. Closed Sun. Slightly rough and utterly traditional bar, which has been run for more than forty years by the no-nonsense Signora Leli. Great for an inexpensive glass, if you don't mind being the only customer who isn't a Venetian male.

# The Canal Grande

The Canal Grande is Venice's high street, and divides the city in half, with three sestieri to the west and three to the east. With the completion of the new bridge to link the bus and train stations, four **bridges** will cross the waterway – the others being at the train station, Rialto and Accademia – but a number of **gondola traghetti** provide additional crossing points at regular intervals, as does the #1 **vaporetto**, which slaloms from one bank to the other along its entire length. The Canal Grande is almost four kilometres long and varies in width between thirty and seventy metres; it is, however, surprisingly shallow, at no point much exceeding five metres.

The section that follows is principally a selection of **Canal Grande palaces** – the churches and other public buildings that you can see from the vaporetto are covered in the appropriate geographical sections.

## The Left Bank

If you come into Venice by train, your first sight of the Canal Grande will be from the upper stretch of its left bank, with the vaporetto landing stages directly in front. To the right is the newest of the Canal Grande's four bridges, the **Ponte Calatrava**, which connects to the bus station. Downstream lies the **Ponte degli Scalzi**, successor of an iron structure put up by the Austrians in 1858–60; like the one at the Accademia, it was replaced in the early 1930s to give the new steamboats sufficient clearance.

### Palazzo Labia

The boat passes two churches, the Scalzi and San Geremia, before the first of the major palaces comes into view – the Palazzo Labia (completed c.1750). The main facade of the building stretches along the Cannaregio canal, but from the Canal Grande you can see how the side wing wraps itself round the campanile of the neighbouring church – such interlocking is common in Venice, where maximum use has to be made of available space.

### Palazzo Vendramin-Calergi

Not far beyond the unfinished church of San Marcuola stands the Palazzo Vendramin-Calergi. Begun by Mauro Codussi at the very end of the fifteenth century, this was the first Venetian palace built on classical Renaissance lines. The palazzo's most famous resident was Richard Wagner, who died here in February 1883. It's now the home of Venice's casino.

### Ca' d'Oro

The most beguiling palace on the canal is the Ca' d'Oro. (*Ca'* is an abbreviation of *Casa* – house.) Incorporating fragments

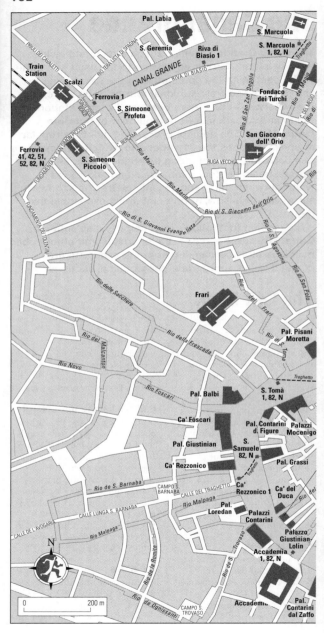

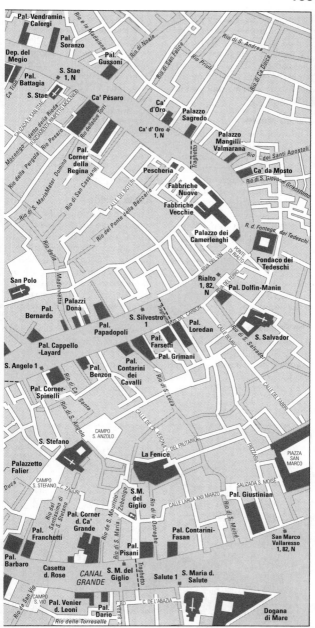

of a thirteenth-century palace that once stood on the site, the Ca' d'Oro was built in the 1420s and 30s, and acquired its nickname – "The Golden House" – from the gilding that used to accentuate much of its carving.

## Ca' da Mosto

The arches of the first floor of the Ca' da Mosto and the carved panels above them are remnants of a thirteenth-century Veneto-Byzantine building, and are thus among the oldest structures to be seen on the Canal Grande. Alvise da Mosto, discoverer of the Cape Verde Islands, was born here in 1432; by the end of that century the palazzo had become the *Albergo del Lion Bianco*, and from then until the nineteenth century it was one of Venice's most popular hotels.

## The Fondaco dei Tedeschi

The huge building just before the Rialto bridge is the Fondaco dei Tedeschi, once headquarters of the city's German merchants. The German traders were the most powerful foreign grouping in the city, and as early as 1228 they were leased a building on this central site. In 1505 the Fondaco burned down; Giorgione and Titian were commissioned to paint the exterior of the new fondaco. The remains of their contribution are now in the Ca' d'Oro. The Fondaco has been renovated several times since the sixteenth century, and is now the main post office.

## Rialto bridge

The famous Ponte di Rialto superseded a succession of wooden structures – one of Carpaccio's *Miracles of the True Cross*, in the Accademia, shows you one of them. The decision to construct a stone bridge was taken in 1524, and eventually the job was awarded to the aptly named Antonio da Ponte, whose top-heavy design was described by Edward Gibbon as "a fine bridge, spoilt by two rows of houses upon it". Until 1854, when the first Accademia bridge was built, this was the only

▼ THE RIALTO BRIDGE

▲ PALAZZO LOREDAN (CENTRE) AND PALAZZO FARSETTI (RIGHT)

point at which the Canal Grande could be crossed on foot.

### Palazzo Loredan and Palazzo Farsetti

The Palazzo Loredan and the Palazzo Farsetti, standing side by side at the end of the Fondamenta del Carbon, are heavily restored Veneto-Byzantine palaces of the thirteenth century. The former was the home of Elena Corner Piscopia, who in 1678 graduated from Padua University, so becoming the first woman ever to hold a university degree. The two buildings are now occupied by the town hall.

### Palazzo Grimani

Work began on the immense Palazzo Grimani in 1559, to designs by Sanmicheli, but was not completed until 1575, sixteen years after his death. Ruskin, normally no fan of Renaissance architecture, made an exception for this colossal palace, calling it "simple, delicate, and sublime".

### The Mocenigo palazzi

Four houses that once all belonged to the Mocenigo family stand side by side on the **Volta del Canal**, as the Canal Grande's sharpest turn is known: the **Palazzo Mocenigo-Nero**, a late sixteenth-century building; the double **Palazzo Mocenigo**, built in the eighteenth century as an extension to the Nero house; and the **Palazzo Mocenigo Vecchio**, a Gothic palace remodelled in the seventeenth century. Byron and his menagerie – a dog, a fox, a wolf and a monkey – lived in the Mocenigo-Nero palace for a couple of years. Much of his time was taken up with a local baker's wife called Margarita Cogni, whose reaction to being rejected by him was to attack him with a table knife and then hurl herself into the Canal Grande.

### Palazzo Grassi

The vast palace round the Volta is the Palazzo Grassi, built in 1748–72 by Massari, who supervised the completion of the Ca' Rezzonico on the

▲ PALAZZO GRASSI

opposite bank. Its first owners were accepted into the ranks of the nobility in return for a hefty contribution to the war effort against the Turks in 1718. Nowadays it's owned by Fiat – hence the sparkling renovation – and is used as an exhibition and conference centre.

### Accademia Bridge

As the larger vaporetti couldn't get under the iron Ponte dell' Accademia built by the Austrians in 1854, it was replaced in 1932 by a wooden one – a temporary measure that became permanent with the addition of a reinforcing steel substructure.

### The Palazzi Barbaro

On the opposite side of the Rio dell'Orso are the twinned Palazzi Barbaro ; the house on the left is early fifteenth-century, the other late seventeenth-century. Henry James, Monet, Whistler, Browning and John Singer Sargent were among the luminaries who stayed in the older Barbaro house in the late nineteenth century as guests of

the Curtis family from Boston. A relative of the painter, Daniel Sargent Curtis bought most of the building in 1885 and it became the centre of American expatriate life in Venice. James finished *The Aspern Papers* here, and used it as a setting for *The Wings of a Dove*.

### Palazzo Corner della Ca' Grande

The palace that used to stand on the site of the Palazzo Corner della Ca' Grande was destroyed when a fire lit to dry out a stock of sugar in the attic ran out of control, an incident that illustrates the dual commercial-residential function of many palaces in Renaissance Venice. Sansovino's replacement was built from 1545 onwards. The rugged stonework of the lower storey – a distinctive aspect of many Roman and Tuscan buildings of the High Renaissance – makes it a prototype for the Ca' Pésaro and Ca' Rezzonico.

### Palazzo Contarini-Fasan

The narrow Palazzo Contarini-Fasan – a mid-fifteenth-century palace with unique wheel tracery on the balconies – is popularly known as "the house of Desdemona", but although the model for Shakespeare's heroine did live in Venice, her association with this house is purely sentimental.

# The Right Bank

Arriving in Venice by road, you come in on the right bank of the Canal Grande at Piazzale Roma, opposite the train station. Orientation is initially difficult, with canals heading off in various directions and no immediate landmark; it's not until the vaporetto swings round by the train station that it becomes obvious that this is the city's main waterway.

### The Fondaco dei Turchi

Having passed the green-domed church of **San Simeone Piccolo**, the end of the elongated campo of **San Simeone Grande** and a procession of nondescript buildings, you come to the Fondaco dei Turchi. A private house from the early thirteenth

century until 1621, it was then turned over to the Turkish traders in the city, who stayed here until 1838. Though it's been over-restored, the building's towers and long water-level arcade give a reasonably precise picture of what a Veneto-Byzantine palace would have looked like.

### Ca' Pésaro

A short distance beyond the church of San Stae stands the thickly ornamented Ca' Pésaro, bristling with diamond-shaped spikes and grotesque heads. Three houses had to be demolished to make room for this palace and its construction lasted half a century – work finished in 1703, long after the death of the architect, Baldassare Longhena.

### Palazzo Corner della Regina

The next large building is the Palazzo Corner della Regina, built in 1724 on the site of the home of Caterina Cornaro, Queen of Cyprus, from whom the palace takes its name. The base of the Biennale archives, it was formerly the Monte di Pietà (municipal pawnshop).

## Venetian palazzi

Virtually all the surviving Canal Grande palaces were built over a span of about 500 years, and in the course of that period the **basic plan** varied very little. The typical Venetian palace has an entrance hall (the **andron**) on the ground floor, and this runs right through the building, flanked by storage rooms. Above comes the mezzanine floor – the small rooms on this level were used as offices or, from the sixteenth century onwards, as libraries or living rooms. On the next floor – often the most extravagantly decorated – you find the **piano nobile**, the main living area, arranged as suites of rooms on each side of a central hall (**portego**), which runs, like the andron, from front to back. The plan of these houses can be read from the outside of the palace, where you'll usually see a cluster of large windows in the centre of the facade, between symmetrically placed side windows. Frequently there is a second *piano nobile* above the first – this generally would have been accommodation for relatives or children (though sometimes it was the main living quarters); the attic would have been used for servants' rooms or storage.

### Rialto markets

Beyond, there's nothing especially engrossing until you reach the Rialto markets, which begin with the neo-Gothic fish market, the **Pescheria**, built in 1907; there's been a fish market here since the fourteenth century. The older buildings that follow it, the **Fabbriche Nuove di Rialto** and (set back from the water) the **Fabbriche Vecchie di Rialto**, are by Sansovino (c.1550) and Scarpagnino (c.1520) respectively.

### Palazzo dei Camerlenghi

The large building at the base of the Rialto bridge is the Palazzo dei Camerlenghi (c.1525), the former chambers of the Venetian exchequer. Debtors could find themselves in the cells of the building's bottom storey – hence the name *Fondamenta delle Prigioni* given to this part of the canalside.

### Palazzo Balbi

The cluster of palaces at the Volta constitutes one of the city's architectural glories. The Palazzo Balbi, on the near side of the Rio di Ca' Fóscari, is the youngest of the group, a proto-Baroque design executed in the 1580s to plans by Alessandro Vittoria, whose sculpture is to be found in many Venetian churches. Nicolò Balbi is reputed to have been so keen to see his palace finished that he moored a boat alongside the building site so that he could watch the work progressing – and died of a chill caught by sleeping in it.

▲ CA' FÓSCARI

### Ca' Fóscari

On the opposite bank stands the Ca' Fóscari (c.1435). The largest private house in Venice at the time of its construction, it was the home of one of the more colourful figures of Venetian history, Doge Francesco Fóscari, whose extraordinarily long term of office (34 years) came to an end with his forced resignation. Venice's university now owns the building, which has been undergoing major restoration for several years.

### The Palazzi Giustinian

Adjoining Ca' Fóscari are the Palazzi Giustinian, a pair of palaces built in the mid-fifteenth century for two brothers who wanted attached but self-contained houses. For a while one of the Palazzi Giustinian was Wagner's home – it was here that he wrote the second act of *Tristan und Isolde*, inspired in part by a nocturnal gondola ride.

## Ca' Rezzonico

A little farther on comes Longhena's gargantuan Ca' Rezzonico. It was begun in 1667 as a commission from the Bon family, but they were obliged to sell the still unfinished palace to the Rezzonico, a family of Genoese bankers who were so rich they could afford not just to complete the palazzo but to tack a ballroom onto the back as well. Among its subsequent owners was Pen Browning, whose father Robert died here in 1889.

## Palazzo Venier dei Leoni

The Venier family, one of Venice's great dynasties (they produced three doges, including the commander of the Christian fleet at Lépanto), had their main base just beyond the Campo San Vio. In 1759 the Veniers began rebuilding their home, but the Palazzo Venier dei Leoni, which would have been the largest palace on the canal, never progressed further than the first storey – hence its alternative name, Palazzo Nonfinito. The stump of the building and the platform on which it is raised (itself an extravagant and novel feature) are occupied by the Guggenheim Collection of modern art.

## Palazzo Dario

The one domestic building of interest between here and the end of the canal is the miniature Palazzo Dario, compared by Henry James to "a house of cards". The palace was built in the late 1480s, and the multicoloured marbles of the facade are characteristic of the work of the Lombardo family.

## The Dogana di Mare

The focal point of this last stretch of the canal is Longhena's masterpiece, Santa Maria della Salute (see p.80), after which comes the Dogana di Mare (Customs House), the Canal Grande's full stop. The figure which swivels in the wind on top of the Dogana's gold ball is said by most to represent Fortune, though others identify it as Justice.

▼ DOGANA DI MARE

# The northern islands

A trip out to the main islands lying to the north of Venice – **San Michele, Murano, Burano** and **Torcello** – will reveal the origins of the glass and lace work touted in so many of the city's shops, and give you a glimpse of the origins of Venice itself, embodied in Torcello's magnificent cathedral of Santa Maria dell'Assunta.

To get to the northern islands, the main **vaporetto stop** is **Fondamente Nove** (or Nuove), as most of the island services start here or call here. (You can hop on elsewhere in the city, of course – but make sure that the boat is going towards the islands, not away from them.) For **San Michele and Murano only**, the circular #41 and #42 vaporetti both run every twenty minutes from Fondamente Nove, circling Murano before heading back towards Venice; the #41 follows an anticlockwise route around the city, the #42 a clockwise route. For **Murano, Burano and Torcello** the #LN (Laguna Nord) leaves every half-hour from Fondamente Nove for most of the day (hourly early in the morning and evenings), calling first at Murano-Faro before heading on to Mazzorbo and Burano, from where it proceeds, via Treporti, to Punta Sabbioni and the Lido. A shuttle boat runs every half-hour between Burano and Torcello.

## San Michele

The high brick wall around the island of San Michele gives way by the landing stage to the elegant white facade of **San Michele in Isola**, designed by Mauro Codussi in 1469. With this building Codussi quietly revolutionized the architecture of Venice, advancing the principles of Renaissance design in the city and introducing the use of Istrian stone as a material for facades. Easy to carve yet resistant to water, Istrian stone had long been used for damp courses, but never before had anyone clad the entire front of a building in it.

The main part of the island, through the cloisters, is covered by the **cemetery** of Venice

(daily: summer 7.30am–6pm; winter 7.30am–4pm),

▼ SAN MICHELE CEMETERY

established here by a Napoleonic decree which forbade further burials in the centre of the city. Space is at a premium, and most of the Catholic dead of Venice lie here in cramped conditions for just ten years or so, when their bones are dug up and removed to an ossuary, and the vacated plot is recycled. The city's Protestants, being less numerous, are permitted to stay in their sector indefinitely. In this Protestant section (no. XV) Ezra Pound's grave is marked by a simple slab with his name on it. Adjoining is the Greek and Russian Orthodox area (no. XIV), including the gravestones of Igor and Vera Stravinsky and the more elaborate tomb of Serge Diaghilev.

## Murano

Murano nowadays owes its fame entirely to its **glass-blowing industry**, and its main fondamente are crowded with shops selling the fruit of the furnaces, some of it fine, most of it repulsive and some of it laughably pretentious. You'll see little in the showrooms to equal the remarkable work on display in the Murano glass museum, and even that takes second place to the island's beautiful main church.

From the Colonna vaporetto stop (the first after San Michele) you step onto the Fondamenta dei Vetrai, traditionally the core of the glass industry (as the name suggests) and now the principal tourist trap. Towards the far end is the Dominican

▲ SANTI MARIA E DONATO

church of **San Pietro Martire** (daily 9am–noon & 3–6pm), one of only two churches still in service on the island (compared with seventeen when the Republic fell in 1797). Begun in 1363 but largely rebuilt after a fire in 1474, its main interest lies with its pair of paintings by Giovanni Bellini.

The seventeenth-century Palazzo Giustinian, formerly home of the Bishop of Torcello, now houses the **Museo del Vetro** (April–Oct 10am–5pm; Nov–March 10am–4pm; closed Wed; €4 or Musei delle Isole card – see p.171). Featuring pieces dating back to the first century and examples of Murano glass from the fifteenth century onwards, the museum exerts a fascination even if you can't read the Italian labels.

### Venetian glass

Because of the risk of fire, Venice's glass furnaces were moved to Murano from central Venice in 1291, and thenceforth all possible steps were taken to keep the secrets of the trade locked up on the island. Although Muranese workers had by the seventeenth century gained some freedom of movement, for centuries prior to that any glass-maker who left Murano was proclaimed a traitor, and a few were even hunted down. A fifteenth-century visitor judged that "in the whole world there are no such craftsmen of glass as here", and the Muranese were masters of every aspect of their craft. They were producing spectacles by the start of the fourteenth century, monopolized the European manufacture of mirrors for a long time, and in the early seventeenth century became so proficient at making coloured crystal that a decree was issued forbidding the manufacture of false gems out of glass, as many were being passed off as authentic stones. The traditional style of Murano glass, typified by the multicoloured floral chandeliers sold in showrooms on Murano and round the Piazza, is still very much in demand. However, in recent years there's been turmoil in the glass industry, due to an inundation of cheap Murano-style tableware and ornaments from Asia and eastern Europe. Few of Murano's 250 glass companies remain in Venetian hands – the long-established firm of Salviati is French-owned, and even Venini has been bought out, by the Royal Copenhagen company.

Perhaps the finest single item is the dark blue Barovier marriage cup, dating from around 1470; it's on show in room 1 on the first floor, along with some splendid Renaissance enamelled and painted glass. A separate display, with some captions in English, covers the history of Murano glass techniques – look out for the extraordinary *Murine in Canna*, the method of placing different coloured rods together to form an image in cross-section.

The other Murano church, and the main reason for visiting the island today, is **Santi Maria e Donato** (daily 8am–noon & 4–7pm). It was founded in the seventh century but rebuilt in the twelfth, and is one of the lagoon's best examples of Veneto-Byzantine architecture – the ornate rear apse being particularly fine. The glories of the interior are its mosaic floor (dated 1141 in the nave) and the arresting twelfth-century mosaic of the Madonna in the apse.

## Burano

After the peeling plaster and eroded stonework of the other lagoon settlements, the small, brightly painted houses of Burano come as something of a surprise. Local tradition says that the colours once enabled each fisherman to identify his house from out at sea, but now the colours are used simply for pleasant effect. While many of the men of Burano still depend on the lagoon for their livelihoods, the women's lives are given over to the production and sale of **lace**, and the shops lining the narrow street leading into the village from the vaporetto stop are full of the stuff. Making Burano-point and Venetian-point lace is extremely

exacting work, both highly skilled and mind-bendingly repetitive, taking an enormous toll on the eyesight. Each woman specializes in one particular stitch, and as there are seven stitches in all, each piece is passed from woman to woman during its construction. An average-size table centre requires about a month of work.

Lacemaking is still taught at Burano's **Scuola dei Merletti** (April–Oct 10am–5pm; Nov–March 10am–4pm; closed Tues; €4 or Musei delle Isole card – see p.171), on Piazza Baldassare Galuppi. This scuola is simply a school rather than a confraternity-cum-guild (unlike all other craftspeople in Venice, the lacemakers had no guild to represent them, perhaps because the workforce was exclusively female) and it was opened in 1872, when the indigenous crafting of lace had declined so

▼ THE LACE MUSEUM

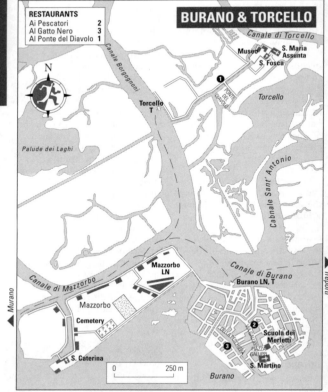

**RESTAURANTS**
| Ai Pescatori | 2 |
| Al Gatto Nero | 3 |
| Al Ponte del Diavolo | 1 |

**BURANO & TORCELLO**

Canale di Torcello
Museo — S. Maria Assunta
S. Fosca
Canale Borgognoni
Torcello T
PONTE DEL DIAVOLO
Torcello
Palude dei Laghi
Canale Sant' Antonio
Canale di Mazzorbo
Mazzorbo LN
Canale di Burano
Burano LN, T
Murano
Mazzorbo
Cemetery
Scuola dei Merletti
PIAZZA GALUPPI
S. Caterina
S. Martino
Burano
treporti

0 — 250 m

far that it was left to one woman, Francesca Memo, to transmit the necessary skills to a younger generation. Pieces produced here are displayed in the attached **museum**, along with specimens dating back to the sixteenth century; after even a quick tour you'll have no problems distinguishing the real thing from the machine-made and imported lace that fills the Burano shops.

Opposite the lace school stands the church of **San Martino** (daily 8am–noon & 3–7pm), with its drunken

campanile; inside, on the second altar on the left, you'll find a fine *Crucifixion* by Giambattista Tiepolo.

### Torcello

Torcello has now come full circle. Settled by the very first refugees from the mainland in the fifth century, it became the seat of the Bishop of Altinum in 638 and in the following year its cathedral – the oldest building in the lagoon – was founded. By the fourteenth century its population had peaked at around twenty thousand, but

Torcello's canals were now silting up, malaria was rife, and the ascendancy of Venice was imminent. By the end of the fifteenth century Torcello was largely deserted and today only about thirty people remain in residence.

A Veneto-Byzantine building dating substantially from 1008, the **Cattedrale di Santa Maria dell'Assunta** (daily: April–Oct 10.30am–6pm; Nov–March 10am–4.30pm; €3; joint ticket with museum €4, or €6 with museum and campanile) has evolved from a church founded in the seventh century, of which the crypt and the circular foundations in front of the facade have survived. The dominant tones of the interior come from pink brick, gold-based mosaics and the watery green-grey marble of its columns and panelling, which together cast a cool light on the richly patterned eleventh-century mosaic floor. In the apse a stunning twelfth-century mosaic of the Madonna and Child looks down from above a frieze of the Apostles, dating from the middle of the previous century. Below the window, at the Madonna's feet, is a much restored image of St Heliodorus, the first Bishop of Altinum. It makes an interesting comparison with the gold-plated face mask on his sarcophagus in front of the high altar, another seventh-century vestige. Mosaic work from the ninth and eleventh centuries adorns the chapel to the right of the high altar, while the other end of the cathedral is dominated by the tumultuous mosaic of the Apotheosis of Christ and the Last Judgement – created in the twelfth century, but renovated in the nineteenth. Ruskin described the **view**

from the campanile as "one of the most notable scenes in this wide world", a verdict you can test for yourself, as the campanile has now been reinforced, cleaned and reopened, after thirty years' service as a pigeon-coop.

Torcello's other church, **Santa Fosca** (same hours as cathedral; free), was built in the eleventh and twelfth centuries for the body of the martyred St Fosca, brought to Torcello from Libya some time before 1011 and now resting under the altar. The bare interior exudes a calmness which no number of visitors can quite destroy.

In the square outside sits the curious **chair of Attila**, perhaps once the throne of Torcello's judges in its earliest days. Behind it, the well-laid-out **Museo di Torcello** (Tues–Sun: April–Oct 10.30am–5.30pm;

▼ SANTA MARIA DELL'ASSUNTA

Nov–March 10am–4.30pm; €2 or joint ticket with cathedral) includes thirteenth-century beaten gold figures, jewellery, mosaic fragments and a mish-mash of pieces relating to the history of the area.

## Shops: Murano glass

### Barovier & Toso
Fondamenta Vetrai 28, ⊛www.barovier.com. This is a family-run firm which can trace its roots back to the fourteenth century. Predominantly traditional designs.

### Berengo Fine Arts
Fondamenta Vetrai 109a & Fondamenta Manin 68. Open daily. Berengo has pioneered a new approach to Venetian glass manufacture, with foreign artists' designs being vitrified by Murano glass-blowers.

### Domus Vetri d'Arte
Fondamenta Vetrai 82. Open daily. Stocks work by the major postwar Venetian glass designers,

▼MURANO GLASS

artists such as Barbini, Ercole Moretti and Carlo Moretti.

### Murano Collezioni
Fondamenta Manin 1c. Outlet for work from the Venini, Moretti and Barovier & Toso factories.

### Penso Davide
Riva Longa 48. The jewellery sold here is both manufactured and designed by the firm, which specializes in giving a new slant to traditional Murano styles. You can watch glass pieces being made in the shop.

### Venini
Fondamenta Vetrai 47, ⊛www.venini.com. One of the more adventurous producers, Venini often employs designers from other fields of the applied arts.

## Shops: Burano lace

### Scuola dei Merletti
Piazza Baldassare Galuppi. The lace here is expensive, but not to a degree that's disproportionate to the hours and labour that go into making it. Be warned that most of the far cheaper stuff that's sold from Burano's open-air stalls is machine-made outside Italy. The Scuola's lace, on the other hand, is the finest handmade material.

## Restaurants

### Ai Pescatori
Via Galuppi 373, Burano ☎041.730.650. Closed Wed. One of the top choices on Burano. Seafood risotto and moderately priced fish dishes predominate.

Open till 11pm, though like other places on the island it closes earlier at slack periods.

### Al Gatto Nero

Fondamenta Giudecca 88, Burano. Closed Mon. Plain but dependably fine local trattoria, just a few minutes' walk from the busy Via Galuppi, opposite the Pescheria. Max, the owner, is a keen fisherman, and what he doesn't know about the marine delicacies of Venice isn't worth knowing.

### Al Ponte del Diavolo

Fondamenta Borgognoni 10/11, Torcello ☎041.730.401. Lunch daily except Wed, booking essential at weekends. Open evenings for group bookings only. The pleasantest restaurant on Torcello, just before the bridge it takes its name from, on the canal leading from the boat to the cathedral. Delightful shaded terrace overlooking the garden. Prices are moderate, unlike at the much-hyped *Locanda Cipriani* near the cathedral.

### Busa alla Torre

Campo S. Stefano 3, Murano ☎041.739.662. Closed Mon. In the opinion of many, this place serves the best fish on Murano. Try the two-course lunch menu for €12.50, excluding drinks.

▼ AL GATTO NERO

# The southern islands

The section of the lagoon to the south of the city,
enclosed by the long islands of the **Lido** and
**Pellestrina**, has fewer outcrops of solid land than its
northern counterpart. The nearer islands are the more
interesting: the Palladian churches of **San Giorgio** and
**La Giudecca** (linked by the #82 vaporetto) are among
Venice's most significant Renaissance monuments,
while the alleyways of La Guidecca are full of reminders
of the city's manufacturing past. The Venetian tourist
industry began with the development of the **Lido**, which
has now been eclipsed by the city itself as a holiday
destination, yet still draws thousands of people to its
beaches each year. A visit to the Armenian island, **San
Lazzaro degli Armeni**, makes an absorbing afternoon's round trip, and if you've a bit more time to spare
you could undertake an expedition to the fishing town
of **Chioggia**, at the southern extremity of the lagoon.
The farther-flung settlements along the route to
Chioggia may have seen more glorious days, but the
voyage out there from the city is a pleasure in itself.

## San Giorgio Maggiore

Palladio's church of San Giorgio
Maggiore (daily: May–Sept
9am–12.30pm & 2.30–6.30pm;
Oct–April 2.30–5pm), facing
the Palazzo Ducale across the

Bacino di San Marco, is one of
the most prominent and familiar
of all Venetian landmarks. It is a
startling building, both on the
outside and inside, where white
stucco is used to dazzling effect –

LA GIUDECCA & SAN GIORGIO MAGGIORE

▲ SAN GIORGIO MAGGIORE

"Of all the colours, none is more proper for churches than white; since the purity of colour, as of the life, is particularly gratifying to God," wrote Palladio. Two outstanding pictures by **Tintoretto** hang in the chancel: *The Last Supper*, perhaps the most famous of all his works, and *The Fall of Manna*. They were painted as a pair in 1592–94 – the last two years of the artist's life, and a *Deposition* of the same date is in the Cappella dei Morti (through the door on the right of the choir). The door on the left of the choir leads to the **campanile** (€3), the best vantage point in all of Venice.

The adjoining monastery – now occupied by the **Fondazione Giorgio Cini**,

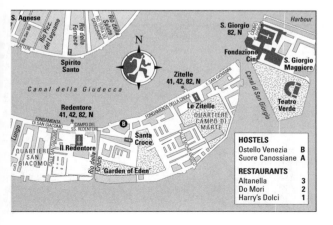

| HOSTELS | |
|---|---|
| Ostello Venezia | B |
| Suore Canossiane | A |

| RESTAURANTS | |
|---|---|
| Altanella | 3 |
| Do Mori | 2 |
| Harry's Dolci | 1 |

which runs various arts research institutes, a naval college and a craft school here – is one of the architectural wonders of the city, featuring two beautiful cloisters and a magnificent refectory by Palladio. Exhibitions are regularly held at the Fondazione; at other times the gatekeeper might allow you a quick look around.

## La Giudecca

In the earliest records of Venice the chain of islets now called La Giudecca was known as Spina Longa, a name clearly derived from its shape. The modern name might refer to the Jews (*Giudei*) who lived here from the late thirteenth century until their removal to the Ghetto, but is most likely to originate with the two disruptive noble families who in the ninth century were shoved into this district to keep them out of mischief (*giudicati* means "judged"). Giudecca grew into the city's industrial inner suburb: Venice's public transport boats used to be made here; an asphalt factory and a distillery were once neighbours at the western end; and the matting

industry, originating in the nineteenth century, kept going here until 1950. However, the semi-dereliction of the present-day island is a potent emblem of Venice's loss of economic self-sufficiency. Swathes of La Giudecca are now purely residential areas, but in this respect things are looking up, with a spate of housing developments and ancillary social facilities being funded in recent years. In no other part of Venice are you as likely to see a site occupied by cranes and bulldozers, and the chances are about even that they'll be putting something up rather than pulling it down.

The first vaporetto stop after San Giorgio Maggiore is close to the tiny church of the **Zitelle** (open for Mass only, Sun 10am–noon), which was built in 1582–86 from plans worked out some years earlier by Palladio, albeit for a different site. La Giudecca's main monument, beyond the tug-boats' mooring and the youth hostel (once a granary), is the Franciscan church of **Il Redentore** (Mon–Sat

▼INTERIOR OF IL REDENTORE

▲ MULINO STUCKY

10am–5pm, Sun 1–5pm; €2 or Chorus Pass – see p.171), designed by Palladio in 1577. In 1575–76, Venice suffered an outbreak of plague which killed nearly fifty thousand people – virtually a third of the city's population. The Redentore was built by the Senate in thanks for Venice's deliverance, and every year until the downfall of the Republic the doge and his senators attended a Mass here to renew their declaration of gratitude, walking to the church over a pontoon bridge from the Záttere. This is the most sophisticated of Palladio's church projects, but an appreciation of its subtleties is difficult, as a rope prevents visitors going beyond the nave. The best paintings in the church are in the sacristy, which is usually closed on Saturday and Sunday.

At the far end of the island looms the colossal **Mulino Stucky**. With the development of the industrial sector at Marghera (on the mainland) after World War I, the Stucky flour mill went into a nose dive, and in 1954 it closed. Since then its future has been a perennially contentious issue –

it's now being restored for use as a convention centre and hotel.

## The Lido

The Lido was an unspoilt strip of land until the latter part of the nineteenth century. Byron used to gallop his horses across its fields every day, and as late as 1869 Henry James could describe the island as "a very natural place". Before the century was out, however, it had become the smartest bathing resort in Italy, and although it's no longer as chic as it was, there's less room on its beaches now than ever before. Unless you're staying at one of the flashy hotels that stand shoulder to shoulder along the seafront, or are prepared to rent one of their beach huts for the day, you'll have to content yourself with the less groomed **public beaches** at the northern and southern ends of the island. The northern beach is twenty minutes' walk from the vaporetto stop at Piazzale Santa Maria Elisabetta; the southern one, right by the municipal golf course, necessitates a bus journey from the Piazzale, and is consequently less of a crush.

The green-domed Santa Maria della Vittoria might be

▲ LIDO LANDING STAGE

the most conspicuous Lido monument on the lagoon side of the island (unless you count the huge Campari sign) but at close quarters it's revealed as a thoroughly abject thing. In the vicinity of the Piazzale only the **Fortezza di Sant'Andrea** is of much interest, and you have to admire it from a distance across the water – you get a good view from the church and Franciscan monastery of **San Nicolò**. A stroll along the nearby Via Cipro (facing the San Nicolò vaporetto stop) will bring you to the entrance to Venice's **Jewish cemetery** (guided tour in English every month except Oct, Sun 2.30pm; €8), which was founded in 1386 and in places has fallen into atmospheric decay.

## From the Lido to Chioggia

The trip across the lagoon to Chioggia is a more protracted business than simply taking the land bus from Piazzale Roma, but it will give you a curative dose of salt air and an understanding of the lagoon. From Gran Viale Santa Maria Elisabetta – the main street from

the Lido landing stage to the sea front – the more or less hourly #11 bus goes down to Alberoni, where it drives onto a ferry for the five-minute hop to Pellestrina; the 10km to the southern tip of Pellestrina are covered by road, and then you switch from the bus to a steamer for the 25-minute crossing to Chioggia. The entire journey takes about eighty minutes, and costs €5 for a one-way through-ticket, including the cost of the hop from San Zaccaria to the Lido – but be sure to check the timetable carefully at Gran Viale Santa Maria Elisabetta, as not every #11 bus goes all the way to Chioggia.

The quickest way back to Venice is by bus (€4) from the Duomo or Sottomarina to Piazzale Roma, but it's only about twenty minutes quicker than the island-hop route, and ACTV passes (see p.169) are not valid, as this is an extra-urban bus service.

The fishing village of **Malamocco**, about 5km into the expedition, is the successor of the ancient settlement called Metamauco, which in the eighth century was the capital of the lagoon confederation. In 1107 the old town was destroyed by a tidal wave; rebuilt Malamocco's most appealing building – the church's scaled-down replica of the Campanile of San Marco – can be seen without getting off the bus.

Fishing and the production of fine pillow-lace are the mainstays of life in the village of **Pellestrina**, which is strung out along nearly a third of the ten kilometres of the next island. There's one remarkable structure here, but you get the best view of it as the boat crosses to Chioggia. This is the **Murazzi**, the colossal walls of Istrian boulders, 4km long and 14m thick at the base, which were constructed at the sides of the Porto di Chioggia to protect Venice from the battering of the sea.

**Chioggia** is the second largest settlement in the lagoon after Venice, and one of Italy's busiest fishing ports. The boat sets you down at the Piazzetta Vigo, at the head of the Corso del Popolo, the principal street in Chioggia's grid-iron layout, which runs down to the cathedral, passing close to the **fish market**, the best in the whole lagoon. Inside the **cathedral**, the chapel to the left of the chancel contains half a dozen good eighteenth-century paintings, including one attributed to Tiepolo; they're all but invisible, a drawback that you might regard as a blessing in view of the subjects depicted – *The Torture of Boiling Oil*, *The Torture of the Razors*, *The Beheading of Two Martyrs*, and so on. Buses run from the cathedral to **Sottomarina**, Chioggia's downmarket answer to Venice's Lido.

### San Lazzaro degli Armeni

Visitors received daily from 3.20pm to 5pm; the connecting #20 motoscafo leaves San Zaccaria at 3.10pm and returns to take you back at the end of the tour; €6. No foreign community has a longer pedigree in Venice than the Armenians, whose presence is most conspicuously signalled by the island of San Lazzaro degli Armeni, identifiable from the city by the onion-shaped summit of its campanile. Tours are conducted by one of the priests who currently live in the

▼SAN LAZZARO DEGLI ARMENI

island's **monastery**, and you can expect him to be trilingual, at the very least. Reflecting the encyclopedic interests of its occupants, the monastery is in places like a whimsically arranged museum: at one end of the old **library**, for example, a mummified Egyptian body is laid out near the sarcophagus in which it was found, while at the other is a teak and ivory throne that once seated the governor of Delhi. The monastery's collection of precious manuscripts and books – the former going back to the fifth century – is another highlight of the visit, occupying a modern rotunda in the heart of the complex. Elsewhere you'll see antique metalwork, extraordinarily intricate Chinese ivory carvings, a gallery of paintings by Armenian artists, a ceiling panel by the young Giambattista Tiepolo, and Canova's figure of Napoleon's infant son, which sits in the chamber in which Byron studied while lending a hand with the preparation of an Armenian–English dictionary. If you're looking for an unusual present, you could buy something at the monastery's shop: the old maps and prints of Venice are a bargain.

# Restaurants

## Altanella

Calle delle Erbe 270, Giudecca ☎041.522.7780. Closed Mon & Tues. Run by the same family for three generations, this mid-range restaurant is highly recommended for its fish dishes and the terrace overlooking the island's central canal. No credit cards. Booking essential.

## Do Mori

Fondamenta Sant'Eufemia 588, Giudecca ☎041.522.5452. Closed Sun. Serves humble pizzas as well as classier fare, with the emphasis, as ever, on fish. For a meal with a view, it can't be bettered.

## Harry's Dolci

Fondamenta S. Biagio 773, Giudecca ☎041.522.4844. Closed Tues. Despite the name, sweets aren't the only things on offer here – the kitchen of this offshoot of *Harry's Bar* is rated by many as the equal of its ancestor. It's less expensive than *Harry's Bar*, but you're nonetheless talking about a place where the cheapest set menu will cost you around €55 a head, drink excluded. Still, if you want to experience Venetian culinary refinement at its most exquisite, this is it.

# Accommodation

# Accommodation

# Hotels

Venice has around two hundred **hotels**, ranging from spartan one-star joints that can charge in excess of €120 per night, such is the level of demand, to five-star establishments costing €900 and upwards; what follows is a run-down on the best choices in all categories. Though there are some typical anomalies, the star system is a broadly reliable indicator of quality, but always bear in mind that you pay through the nose for your proximity to the Piazza.

**Breakfast** is nearly always included in the hotel room rate; if it isn't, you should anticipate a charge of at least €7 for a jug of coffee and a croissant. Except where specified otherwise, prices given in the following listings are for rooms in high season.

Recent changes in the local regulations governing the provision of tourist accommodation have led to a proliferation of **bed and breakfast** establishments in the city. The smartest of these places, usually operating under the title **locanda**, are in effect small family-run guesthouses, offering good-value rooms, attentive service, and often a very attractive location. *Locande* usually offer a standard of accommodation equivalent to three- or even four-star hotels (24–hour room service is just about the only facility they don't provide), but often at considerably lower cost.

You can find **information** for both *locande* and hotels on the tourist office's website ⓦwww.turismovenezia.it and also on ⓦwww.veniceby.com.

## San Marco: North of the Piazza

▸ SEE MAP ON P65

**Ai Do Mori Calle Larga S. Marzo, S. Marco 658** ☏041.520.4817, ⓦwww .hotelaidomori.com. Very friendly, and

---

### Booking a room

**High season** in Venice covers most of the year – officially it runs from March 15 to November 15 and then from December 21 to January 6, but many places don't recognize the existence of a low season any more. If you intend to stay in the city at any time during the above periods (or Carnevale), it's wise to book your place at least three months in advance, and for June, July and August it's virtually obligatory to reserve half a year ahead.

Should you bowl into town unannounced in high summer, the **booking offices** (see below) may be able to dig out something in Mestre, on the mainland. During the winter it may well be possible to find a reduced-rate room, but it might involve a bit of legwork, as some hotels, especially the less expensive ones, close down from November to February or March (reopening briefly for Christmas and New Year in many cases).

**Booking offices** are located at the **train station** (daily: summer 8am–9pm; winter 8am–7pm); on the **Tronchetto** (9am–8pm); in the multistorey car park at **Piazzale Roma** (9am–9pm); at **Marco Polo airport** (summer 9am–7pm; winter noon–7pm); and at the **autostrada's Venice exit** (8am–8pm). They only deal with hotels (not hostels) and take a deposit that's deductible from your first night's bill.

situated a few paces off the Piazza, this is a top recommendation for budget travellers. The top-floor room has a private terrace looking over the roofs of the Basilica and the Torre dell'Orologio, and is one of the most attractive (and, of course, expensive) one-star rooms in the city. Non smoking. Doubles €90–135.

**Casa Petrarca** Calle dei Fabbri, S. Marco 4386 ⊕ & ⓟ041.520.0430. A very hospitable one-star, one of the cheapest hotels within a stone's throw of the Piazza – but make sure you phone first, as it only has seven rooms, including a tiny single. No credit cards. Doubles from around €120.

**Noemi** Calle delle Schiavini, S. Marco 909 ⊕041.523.8144, ⓦwww.hotelnoemi .com. *Noemi* is right in the thick of the action, just a minute's walk north of the Piazza, but its prices are lower than most rival one-stars. Decor is eighteenth-century Venetian and half its 16 rooms have private bathrooms. Doubles from around €100.

**Orseolo** Corte Zorzi S. Marco 1083, ⊕041.520.4827, ⓦwww.locandaorseolo .com. Friendly and recently opened family-run locanda abutting the Orseolo canal, 50m north of the Piazza. Rooms are spacious and light; breakfasts substantial. Entrance is through an iron gate in Campo S. Gallo. Doubles from around €200.

# San Marco: West of the Piazza

▸ SEE MAP ON P.71

**Ala** Campo S. Maria del Giglio, S. Marco 2494 ⊕041.520.8333, ⓦwww.hotelala.it. The three-star family-run *Ala* has spacious rooms (choose between modern and traditional Venetian) and a perfect location, on a square that opens out onto the mouth of the Canal Grande. Often has good special offers. Doubles from around €240.

**Art Deco** Calle delle Botteghe, Campo S. Stefano 2966 ⊕041.277.0558, ⓦwww.locandaartdeco.com. This new three-star *locanda* has a seventeenth-century palazzo setting, but the interior is strewn with 1930s and 40s objects. The pristinely white bedrooms have modern wrought-iron furniture. Doubles from around €160.

**Fiorita** Campiello Nuovo, S. Marco 3457 ⊕041.523.4754, ⓦwww.locandafiorita .com. Welcoming one-star with just ten rooms, so it's crucial to book well in advance. Doubles from around €110.

**Flora** Calle Larga XXII Marzo, S. Marco 2283/a ⊕041.520.5844, ⓦwww .hotelflora.it. This large three-star is very close to the Piazza and has a delightful inner garden. Rooms are beautifully decorated with period pieces, though some are a little cramped. Doubles from around €230.

**Gritti Palace** Calle Larga del Giglio, S. Marco 2467 ⊕041.794.611, ⓦwww .starwood.com/grittipalace. One of Venice's most prestigious addresses, reeking of old-regime opulence. No doubles under €380 per night, and the plushest suite will set you back well over a thousand euros.

**Kette** Piscina S. Moisè, S. Marco 2053 ⊕041.520.7766, ⓟ041.522.8964, ⓦwww.hotelkette.com. A four-star favourite with the upper-bracket tour companies, mainly on account of its quiet location, in an alleyway parallel to Calle Larga XXII Marzo. In season there's nothing under €230, but out of season prices are much more reasonable.

**Monaco and Grand Canal** Calle Vallaresso, S. Marco 1325 ⊕041.520.0211, ⓦwww.summithotels .com. Very stylish four-star hotel owned by the Benetton family – try to get one of the ground-floor rooms, which look over to the Salute. Room rates can be as low as €200 out of season, but expect to pay at least double that in summer.

**Novecento** Calle del Dose, S. Marco 2683 ⊕041.241.3765, ⓦwww .locandanovecento.it. Boutique-style three-star hotel with nine individually decorated doubles with bathrooms. Styling is ethnic eclectic (floor cushions and Moroccan lamps), and there's a small courtyard for breakfast. Doubles from around €180.

# Dorsoduro

▶ SEE MAP ON P.76

**Accademia Villa Maravege** Fondamenta Bollani, Dorsoduro 1058 ☏041.523.0188, ⊛www.pensioneaccademia.it. Once the Russian embassy, this three-star seventeenth-century villa has a devoted following, not least on account of its garden, which occupies a promontory at the convergence of two canals, with a view of a small section of the Canal Grande. To be sure of a room, get your booking in at least three months ahead. Doubles from around €180.

**Agli Alboretti** Rio Terrà Foscarini, Dorsoduro 884 ☏041.523.0058, ⊛www.aglialboretti.com. Friendly two-star well situated right next to the Accademia. All rooms have air-conditioning and TV. Avoid murky room 19 and you can't go wrong. Doubles from around €170.

**Ca' Pisani** Rio Terà Foscarini, Dorsoduro 979a ☏041.240.1411, ⊛www .capisanihotel.it. This very glamorous 29-room four-star, just a few metres from the Accademia, created quite a stir when it opened in 2000, chiefly because of its high-class retro look. Taking its cue from the style of the 1930s and 40s, the *Ca' Pisani* makes heavy use of dark wood and chrome, a refreshing break from the Renaissance and Rococo tones that tend to prevail in Venice's upmarket establishments. Highly recommended. Doubles from around €300.

**La Calcina** Záttere ai Gesuati, Dorsoduro 780 ☏041.520.6466, ⊛www.lacalcina .com. Charismatic three-star hotel in the house where Ruskin wrote much of *The Stones of Venice*. From the more expensive rooms you can gaze across to the Redentore, a church that gave him apoplexy. All rooms are no-smoking and have parquet floors – unusual in Venice. No TV or minibar in the rooms – a decision indicative of the desire to maintain the building's character. Its restaurant (see p.88) is good too. Doubles from around €150.

**Messner** Rio Terrà dei Catacumeni, Dorsoduro 216 ☏041.522.7443, ⊛www.hotelmessner.it. In an excellent, quiet location close to the Salute vaporetto stop, the *Messner* has modern, smart rooms and is run by friendly staff. The one-star annexe round the corner past the *Alla Salute* hotel has some doubles for around half the price of those in the smaller but more appealing two-star main building. Doubles from around €115.

**Pausania** Fondamenta Gherardini, Dorsoduro 3942 ☏041.522.2083, ⊛www.hotelpausania.it. This quiet, comfortable and friendly three-star has an excellent location very close to San Barnaba church, just five minutes from the Accademia. Doubles from around €150.

**San Barnaba** Calle del Traghetto, Dorsoduro 2785 ☏041.241.1233, ⊛www.locanda-sanbarnaba.com. Exceptionally pleasant three-star hotel right by the Ca' Rezzonico. Well-equipped rooms – some have eighteenth-century frescoes, and one has an enormous family-size bath. Doubles from around €170.

# San Polo and Santa Croce

▶ SEE MAP ON P.90

**Al Gallo** Calle del Forno, S. Croce 88 ☏041.523.6761, ⊛www.algallo.it. Small family-run three-star, not far from the Frari, with rooms (with and without bath) furnished in the Venetian style. Doubles from around €110.

**Alex** Rio Terrà Frari, S. Polo 2606 ☏ & ☏041.523.1341, ⊛www .hotelalexinvenice.com. A longstanding budget travellers' favourite; the supermarket in front is useful for picnics and breakfasts. No credit cards. Doubles from around €80.

**Ca' Fóscari** Calle della Frescada, Dorsoduro 3888 ☏ & ☏041.522.5817, ⊛www.locandacafoscari.com. Quiet, well decorated and relaxed one-star, tucked away in a micro-alley near S. Tomà. Just 11 rooms (7 without bathroom), so it's quickly booked out. Doubles from around €80.

**Falier** Salizzada S. Pantalon, S. Croce 130 ☏041.710.882, ⊛www.hotelfalier.com.

Neat, sprucely renovated little two-star, very close to San Rocco and the Frari. Doubles from around €180.

**Locanda Salieri Fondamenta Minotto, S. Croce 160 ☎041.710.035, ✉www .hotelsalieri.com.** Exceptionally friendly one-star hotel, on a very picturesque canal-side. Rooms are light and airy. Doubles from around €80.

**San Cassiano-Ca' Favretto Calle della Rosa, S. Croce 2232 ☎041.524.1768, ✉www.sancassiano.it.** Beautiful three-star with some rooms looking across the Canal Grande towards the Ca' d'Oro. Has very helpful staff, a nice courtyard garden and a grand entrance hall. Doubles from around €200.

**Sturion Calle del Sturion, S. Polo 679 ☎041.523.6243, ✉www.locandasturion .com.** This immaculate 11-room three-star has a very long pedigree – the sign of the sturgeon (*sturion*) appears in Carpaccio's *Miracle of the True Cross at the Rialto Bridge* (in the Accademia). It's on a wonderful site a few yards from the Canal Grande, close to the Rialto, but visitors with mobility difficulties should look elsewhere, as the hotel is at the top of three flights of stairs and has no lift. Rates drop considerably in winter. Doubles from around €220.

# Cannaregio

▶ SEE MAP ON P.104

**Abbazia Calle Priuli, Cannaregio 66 ☎041.717.333, ✉www.abbaziahotel .com.** Occupying a former Carmelite monastery (the monks attached to the Scalzi still live in a building adjoining the hotel), the light-filled *Abbazia* provides three-star amenities without losing its air of quasi-monastic austerity. There's a delightful garden too. Doubles from around €150.

**Adua Lista di Spagna, Cannaregio 233/a ☎041.716.184, ☎041.244.0162.** Large one-star with friendly management and benign prices. Around half of the 27 rooms do not have a private bathroom, but the rooms in the annexe all have showers. No credit cards. Doubles from around €70.

**Al Saor Calle Zotti, Cannaregio 3904/a ☎ & ☎041.296.0654, ✉www.alsaor .com.** Friendly B&B, located near the Ca' d'Oro. Five spacious air-conditioned rooms, two of them with cooking facilities. If you stay for more than four nights, the family will take you on a trip round the back canals – a great way to see the city. Doubles from around €90.

**Bernardi Semenzato Calle dell'Oca 4366 ☎041.522.7257, ✉www .hotelbernardi.com.** Very well-priced two-star in a prime location (in a tiny alleyway close to Campo S. Apostoli), with immensely helpful owners who speak excellent English. Has some cheaper rooms with shared bathrooms, and 5 singles for as little as €35 with a shared bathroom. The annexe round the corner has air conditioning. Doubles from around €70.

**Casa Martini Rio Terrà S. Leonardo, Cannaregio 1314 ☎041.717.512, ✉www.casamartini.it.** Delightful small hotel near the Cannaregio canal. Nine pleasantly furnished a/c rooms, with breakfast terrace at the back, and kitchen for guests' use. Doubles from around €130.

**Del Ghetto Campo del Ghetto Novo, Cannaregio 2892 ☎041.275.9292, ✉www.veneziahotels.com.** Friendly nine-room locanda in the heart of the Ghetto. Well-equipped a/c rooms have beautiful features, including wooden floors and old beams. Two rooms have a small balcony. Kosher breakfast. Doubles from around €180.

**Giorgione Calle Larga dei Proverbi, Cannaregio 4587 ☎041.522.5810, ✉www.hotelgiorgione.com.** High-class four-star hotel not far from the Rialto bridge, with a very personal touch – it has been run by the same family for generations. Non-smoking floor, quiet courtyard, pool table, free Internet access, and 76 well-equipped rooms, including rooms for disabled visitors. Free tea and coffee served in the lounge in the afternoon. Doubles from around €270.

**Novo Calle dei Preti, Cannaregio 4529 ☎041.241.1496, ✉www.locandanovo.it.** Newly established locanda in a lovingly restored palazzo near Santi Apostoli. Ten large, well-furnished rooms, some with a/c. Doubles from around €120.

**Villa Rosa** Calle della Misericordia, Cannaregio 389 ☎041.718.976, ⊕www.villarosahotel.com. Clean and fairly large one-star; the rooms here have a/c and private bathrooms – the best even have a small balcony. There is a large terrace at the back for breakfast. Doubles from around €100.

# Central Castello

▶ SEE MAP ON P.115

**Al Leon** Campo SS. Filippo e Giacomo, Castello 4270 ☎041.277.0393, ⊕www.hotelalleon.com. Friendly locanda very close to the Piazza, with 9 pleasantly furnished a/c rooms – not big, but well-equipped. Doubles from around €140.

**Canada** Campo S. Lio, Castello 5659 ☎041.522.9912, ⊕041.523.5852. Well-kept and friendly second-floor two-star; 6 of the 25 rooms have a/c. Book well in advance for the room with a roof terrace. Doubles from around €160.

**Caneva** Corte Rubbi, Castello 5515 ☎041.522.8118, ⊕www.hotelcaneva .com. A well-appointed and peaceful one-star tucked away behind the church of S. Maria della Fava, close to Campo S. Bartolomeo. About half of the 23 rooms have a/c, and some have private bathrooms. Doubles from around €80.

**Casa Querini** Campo S. Giovanni Novo, Castello 4388 ☎041.241.1294, ⊕www.locandaquerini.com. Friendly small locanda occupying parts of two houses in a quiet courtyard near the Piazza. Eleven smallish but nicely furnished a/c rooms. Doubles from around €170.

**Casa Verardo** Calle della Chiesa, Castello 4765 ☎041.528.6127, ⊕www.casaverardo.it. Very fine, newly refurbished three-star hotel just a couple of minutes from San Marco and Campo S. Maria Formosa. Twenty very well-equipped rooms with a breakfast terrace downstairs, a sun lounge at the top and another terrace attached to one of the rooms. Doubles from around €180.

**Danieli** Riva degli Schiavoni, Castello 4196 ☎041.522.6480, ⊕www .luxurycollection.com/danieli. This magnificent Gothic palazzo affords just about the most sybaritic hotel experience on the continent – provided you book a room in the old part of the building, not the modern extension. Cheapest doubles are €735, but with a lagoon view you move towards the €900 mark.

**Doni** Fondamenta del Vin, Castello 4656 ☎ & ⊕041.522.4267. A cosy one-star near San Zaccaria where most of the 13 rooms look over the Rio del Vin or a courtyard, though only 4 of them have a private bathroom. Room 8 is special for its ceiling fresco. Doubles from around €90.

**Locanda Leon Bianco** Corte Leon Bianco, Castello 5629 ☎041.523.3572, ⊕www.leonbianco.it. Friendly and charming three-star in a superb location not far from the Rialto bridge, tucked away beside the decaying Ca' da Mosto. Only 8 rooms, but 3 of them overlook the Canal Grande and 4 of the others are spacious and tastefully furnished in eighteenth-century style – one even has a huge fresco in the mode of Giambattista Tiepolo. A gem of a place. Doubles from around €130.

**Paganelli** Riva degli Schiavoni, Castello 4182 ☎041.522.4324, ⊕www.hotelpaganelli.com. This three-star is a great place to stay, as long as you get one of the rooms on the lagoon side – the ones in the annexe look onto S. Zaccaria, which is a nice enough view, but not really in the same league, though of course they are cheaper. Doubles from around €150.

**Scandinavia** Campo S. Maria Formosa, Castello 5240 ☎041.522.3507, ⊕www.scandinaviahotel.com. Sizeable and comfortable three-star on one of the city's most lively and spacious squares. Decorated mainly in eighteenth-century style (ie lots of Murano glass and floral motifs), it has an unusually wide variety of accommodation, ranging from large suites to rooms with private but not en-suite bathroom. Off-peak prices are considerably lower than high-season. Doubles from around €150.

## Eastern Castello

▶ SEE MAP ON P.124

**Casa Linger Salizzada S. Antonin, Castello 3541** ☎041.528.5920, ✉hotelcasalinger@libero.it. Well off the tourist rat-run, this one-star is a decent budget option, as long as you don't mind the climb to the front door – it's at the top of a very steep staircase. Good-sized rooms with and without bath. No singles. Doubles from around €80.

**Gabrielli Sandwirth Riva degli Schiavoni, Castello 4110** ☎041.523.1580, ⊛www.hotelgabrielli.it. A converted Gothic palace, with a lovely courtyard. Four-star comfort and *Danieli*-style views across the Bacino di San Marco for half the price of the *Danieli*. Doubles start at €250 in low season, going up to around €440 in high season.

**La Residenza Campo Bandiera e Moro, Castello 3608** ☎041.528.5315, ⊛www.venicelaresidenza.com. This four-teenth-century palazzo is a mid-budget gem (in Venetian terms), occupying much of one side of a tranquil square just off the main waterfront. It was once a tad pricier than the average two-star, but the rest of the pack have raised their tariffs in more recent years, making *La Residenza* a top choice. The recently refurbished rooms are spacious (rare at this price) and elegant. Doubles from around €140.

# Apartments

The very high cost of hotel rooms in Venice makes **self-catering** an attractive option – for the price of a week in a cramped double room in a three-star hotel you could book yourself a two-bedroom apartment right in the centre of the city. Many package holiday companies have a few Venetian apartments in their brochures, but you'll get a far better selection if you go to a company that specializes in short-let self-catering accommodation. The two listed below are recommended.

**Italian Breaks** ☎020/8660 0082, ⊛www.italianbreaks.com. This company has a selection of a couple of dozen apartments in Venice, ranging from a one-bed place near the Fondamente Nuove to a four-bedroom apartment with views of the Canal Grande.

**Venetian Apartments** ☎020/8878 1130, ⊛www.venice-rentals.com. By a long way the leader in the field, Venetian Apartments manages holiday accommodation in Rome, Florence and Siena as well as Venice, but Venice is at the heart of an operation that offers more than a hundred apartments in the city, ranging from studios at around €800 per week, through 1- to 4-bedroom apartments to extraordinarily sumptuous palazzi on the Canal Grande that will set you back around €10,000. The properties are immaculately maintained, and the agency provides very friendly backup in Venice itself. It also has an exemplary website, with detailed maps showing the location of each apartment, photographs of virtually every room, ground plans and full rental details.

# Hostels

Venice has a large HI hostel and a few hostels run by religious foundations, which are generally open to tourists during the university's summer vacation – during term time they double as student accommodation.

**Domus Ciliota Calle delle Muneghe, S. Marco 2976** ☎041.520.4888, ⊛www.ciliota.it; map on p.71. Welcoming but expensive mixed hostel-style accommodation, close to Campo S. Stefano. Open mid-June to mid-Sept. Evening meal €14.40. Singles €85, doubles €106.

**Domus Civica Calle Campazzo, S. Polo 3082** ☎041.721.103; map on p.90. A student house in winter, open to travellers from mid-June to Sept. Most rooms are double with running water; showers free; no breakfast; 11.30pm curfew. Single €29.50, double €54, with 20 percent reduction for ISIC card-holders.

**Foresteria Valdese S. Maria Formosa, Castello 5170** ☎041.528.6797, ⊛www.diaconiavaldese.org/venezia; map on p.115. Installed in a wonderful palazzo at the end of Calle Lunga S. Maria Formosa, this is principally a hostel for grown-ups, with occasional school groups. Five large dorms, and four rooms for 2–4 people. It also has a couple of self-catering flats sleeping 4 and 5 people. Reservations by phone only; dorm beds cannot be booked in advance. Registration 9am–1pm & 6–8pm. Prices range from €21 for a dorm bed to €74 for a double room with own bathroom (2 nights minimum).

**Ostello Santa Fosca S. Maria dei Servi, Cannaregio 2372,** ☎041.715.733, ⊛www.santafosca.com; map on p.104. Student-run hostel in an atmospheric former Servite convent in a quiet part of Cannaregio, with dorm beds and double rooms, all with shared bathrooms. Check-in 5–8pm; 12.30pm curfew. Dorm bed €18, €21 per person in smaller rooms. They take bookings one week ahead only, and only by phone; it's essential to book in summer.

**Ostello Venezia Fondamenta delle Zitelle, Giudecca 86** ☎041.523.8211, ☎041.523.5689; map on p.148. The city's HI hostel occupies a superb location looking over to San Marco, but it's run with a certain briskness. Registration opens at 1.30pm in summer and 4pm in winter. Curfew at midnight, chucking-out time 9.30am. Gets so busy in July and August that written reservations must be made by April. Breakfast and sheets included in the price – but remember to add the expense of the boat over to Giudecca (the nearest stop is Zitelle). No kitchen, but full (and excellent) meals for €8.50. €17.50 per bed, breakfast included; HI card necessary, but you can join on the spot for €15.50.

**Suore Canossiane Fondamenta del Ponte Piccolo, Giudecca 428** ☎041.522.2157; map on p.148. Women-only hostel run by nuns, near the Palanca vaporetto stop. Open 6.30–9am & 3–10.30pm; no pre-booking. Dorm bed €15.

Essentials

Essentials

# Arrival

Millions of visitors pour into Venice each year, most of them funnelled through Venice's small Marco Polo airport, on the outskirts of Venice itself, or through Treviso, 30km inland. Arriving by train and coach is painless – but driving into Venice is unmitigated hell in summer.

## By air

Most **scheduled** flights and some charters arrive at **Marco Polo**, around 7km north of Venice, on the edge of the lagoon. Hourly Alilaguna **water-buses** call at Murano, the Lido, the Arsenale and San Marco (€10; journey time 1hr to San Marco), or you could take one of the two road-going **bus services** to the terminal at Piazzale Roma: the ATVO (*Azienda Trasporti Veneto Orientale*) coach, which departs every half-hour and takes around twenty minutes (€3), or the ACTV (*Azienda del Consorzio Trasporti Veneziano*) bus #5, which is equally frequent, usually takes a few minutes longer, but costs just €1. The **ticket office** for all buses is in the arrivals hall; in addition to single tickets, you can also get ACTV passes here (see p.169) – a wise investment. Note that ACTV passes are only valid on the ACTV bus into Venice, not the Alilaguna service nor on the ATVO bus, and that the office will sell you a ticket for the ATVO rather than the ACTV bus unless you make clear your preference for *il cinque* (#5).

The most luxurious means of getting into the city is to take a **water-taxi**. The drivers tout for business in and around the arrivals hall, and will charge in the region of €80 to San Marco, for up to six people. Ordinary **car-taxis** are ranked outside the arrivals hall, and cost about €30 to Piazzale Roma.

**Treviso** airport is used chiefly by **charter** companies, some of which provide a free bus link from the airport into Venice. Ryanair's twice-daily flights use Treviso too, and are met by an ATVO bus service to Venice; the fare is €4.40 single and the journey takes 1hr 10min. Otherwise, take the #6 bus from right outside the arrivals building into Treviso (20min), from where there are very frequent bus and train connections to Venice. Tickets are best bought before you get onto the bus, from the bar across the road; if you buy them from the driver they cost almost twice as much.

Land buses and taxis depart from immediately outside the arrivals hall; a free shuttle bus takes you to the Alilaguna boats and water taxis.

## By road and rail

Arriving by **train**, **coach or bus**, you simply get off at the end of the line. The **Piazzale Roma** bus station and **Santa Lucia** train station (don't get off at Venezia Mestre, which is the last stop on the mainland) are just five minutes' walk from each other at the top of the Canal Grande. The **left-luggage** office at the end of platform 14 at the train station is open from 6am to midnight and charges €3 per item for the first twelve hours, then €2 for each succeeding twelve hours.

# Information

The main **tourist office** – known as the **Venice Pavilion** – occupies the Palazzina del Santi, on the west side of the Giardinetti Reali, within a minute of the Piazza (daily 10am–6pm; ☎041.529.8711, ⓦwww.turismovenezia.it); smaller offices operate at Calle dell'Ascensione 71/f, in the corner of the Piazza's arcades (daily 9am–3.30pm; ☎041.520.8740), the train station (daily 8am–6.30pm; ☎041.529.8727), in the airport arrivals area (Mon–Sat 9.30am–7.30pm;

## The Venice and Rolling Venice cards

Active sightseers should consider investing in a **Venice Card**, which comes in two forms and is valid for either one, three or seven days, with a discount for the under-30s. The **blue** card (1-day €14, €9 with discount; 3-day €29/€22; 7-day €51/€49) gives unlimited access to all ACTV public transport and staffed AmaV toilets, and a few small discounts on admission charges (eg to the Museo Ebraico and the Querini Stampalia gallery). The **orange** card (1-day €28/€18; 3-day €47/€35; 7-day €68/€61) accords the same benefits as the blue card and also gives free access to all the museums covered by the Museum Pass (see p.171), and thus represents a very good deal if you're going to pack a lot into your trip.

You can **buy** Venice Cards from the main tourist office, the Alilaguna office at the airport, the VeLa ticket offices at the train station and Piazzale Roma, the ACTV/Hello Venezia office at Ramo dei Fuseri 1810, or the ASM offices at the San Giuliano and Tronchetto car parks. Alternatively, you can order the card a minimum of 48 hours in advance on ⓦwww.venicecard.com or by calling ☎899.909.090 within Italy (it's a free number), or ☎00.39.041.4747 or ☎00.39.041.2424 from abroad. You will be given a code number which you will need to present when you turn up to collect your ticket from any of the offices listed above.

If you're aged between 14 and 29, you are eligible for a **Rolling Venice** card, which entitles you to discounts at some shops, restaurants, cinemas, museums and exhibitions, plus reductions on some transport services, all of which are detailed in a leaflet that comes with the card. The card costs €2.58, is valid for a year, and is worth buying if you're in town for at least a week and aim to make the most of every minute. The tourist offices have information on it but only the following places issue it: Agenzia Transalpino, at the train station; Servizio Politiche Giovanili, Corte Contarina 1529, San Marco; Agenzia Arte e Storia, Santa Croce 659, near Campo della Lana; Associazione Italiana Alberghi per la Gioventù, Calle del Castelforte 3101, San Polo (near the Scuola di San Rocco); and ACTV/VeLa agencies and offices.

☎041.541.5887), at the multistorey car park at Piazzale Roma (daily 9.30am–6.30pm; ☎041.529.8746) and on the Lido at Gran Viale S.M. Elisabetta 6 (June–Sept daily 9.30am–12.30pm & 3.30–6pm; ☎041.526.5721). The Calle dell'Ascension office is supposed to be the city's main outlet for information on the whole Veneto, but the staff are rarely as helpful as those in the Venice Pavilion.

The English–Italian **magazine** *Un Ospite di Venezia* (ⓦwww.unospitedi-venezia.it), produced fortnightly in summer and monthly in winter, gives up-to-date information on exhibitions, special events and vaporetto timetables – it's free from the main tourist office, and from the receptions of the posher hotels.

# City transport

Apart from services #1 and the #82, the water-buses skirt the city centre, connecting points on the periphery and the outer islands. In many cases the speediest way of getting around is **on foot**. Routes between major sights are sometimes tortuous but distances are extremely short (you can cross the whole city in an hour), and once you've got your general bearings you'll find that navigation is not as daunting as it seems at first. Helpful yellow signs posted high up on streetcorners all over central Venice indicate the main routes to San Marco, Ferrovia (train station) and Rialto.

# Water-buses

There are two basic types of water-bus: the **vaporetti**, which are the lumbering workhorses used on the Canal Grande services (#1 and #82) and other heavily used routes, and the **motoscafi**, which are smaller vessels employed on routes where the volume of traffic isn't as great. The standard fare is €3.50 for a single journey (or €6 for two tickets, to be used before midnight), except for the Laguna Nord boats (to Murano, Burano and Torcello), which cost €8.50 and are valid for twelve hours, and Canal Grande trips on the #1, #3, #4 and #82: on these vaporetti the fare is €5 for any journey stopping anywhere between Piazzale Roma and San Marco Vallaresso, other than a one-stop traghetto hop (see below), in which case the fare is €1.80. The €5 ticket is valid for ninety minutes of travel; other single tickets are valid for just one journey. Children under 4 travel free.

**Tickets** are available from most landing stages, from *tabacchi*, from shops displaying the ACTV sign, at the airport, from the main tourist office, and from the two ACTV public offices – at Piazzale Roma (daily: summer 6am–midnight; winter 6am–8pm) and in Ramo dei Fuseri, close to the northwest corner of the Piazza (Mon–Fri 7.30am–6pm, Sat 7.30am–1pm). In the remoter parts of the city, you may not be able to find anywhere to buy a ticket, particularly after working hours, when the booths at the landing stages tend to close down; tickets can be bought on board at the standard price, as long as you ask the attendant as soon as you get on board; if you delay, you could be liable for a €35 spot-fine on top of the fare.

Unless you intend to walk all day, you'll almost certainly save money by buying some sort of **travel card** as soon as you arrive. ACTV produces a **one-day** (24hr) ticket (€10.50) and a **three-day** (72hr) ticket (€22), which can be used on all ACTV services within Venice (including ACTV land buses from the airport). For seven days of unrestricted travel, you have to buy a Venice Card (see p.168).

If you buy one of these unrestricted travel tickets at the train station or Piazzale Roma it will in all likelihood be automatically **validated** with a time-stamp; the same goes for ordinary tickets. When using a **non-validated** ticket you must validate it before embarking, by inserting it into one of the machines at the entrance to the vaporetto stop or on board the bus (the machines are painted orange); the ticket is valid from that moment, and you need to validate it just once.

## Water-bus services

What follows is a run-through of the most useful services. Be warned that so many services call at San Marco, San Zaccaria, Rialto and the train station that the bus stops at these points are spread out over a long stretch of waterfront, so you might have to walk past several stops before finding the one you need. Services to San Marco will call either at plain San Marco or at the adjacent San Marco Vallaresso. As a further refinement, the San Zaccaria stop, which is as close to the Basilica as the San Marco Vallaresso stop, is sometimes treated as the third San Marco stop.

### #1

The slowest of the water-buses, and the one you'll use most often. It starts at Piazzale Roma, calls at every stop on the Canal Grande except San Samuele, works its way along the San Marco waterfront to Sant'Elena, then goes over to the Lido. The #1 runs every 20min between 5 and 6.30am, every 10min between 6.30am and 9.45pm, and every 20min between 9.45 and 11.45pm. For the night service, see #N.

### #82

This service is the quickest means of getting from the train or bus station down the Canal Grande to San Marco, as it makes fewer stops than the #1. Its clockwise route takes it from San Zaccaria to San Giorgio

Maggiore, Giudecca (Zitelle, Redentore and Palanca), Záttere, San Basilio, Sacca Fisola, Tronchetto, Piazzale Roma, the train station, then down the Canal Grande (usually calling at Rialto, Sant'Angelo, San Tomà, San Samuele and Accademia) to San Marco (Vallaresso); the anticlockwise version calls at the same stops. From Monday to Friday the #82 runs along most of the route (in both directions) every 10min from 6am to 8.30pm, then every 20min until 11pm, but for the section between Rialto and San Marco the bus runs only every 20min through the day and is even less frequent before 8am and after 8.30pm; at weekends the #82 runs every 20min for the whole route. In summer the #82 is extended from San Zaccaria to the Lido. For the night service see #N.

#### #41/42
The circular service, running right round the core of Venice, with a short detour at the northern end to San Michele and Murano. The #41 travels anticlockwise, the #42 clockwise, and both run every 20min from 6.30am until around 8pm, after which the service simply shuttles between Murano and Venice every 10–20min until around 11.30pm.

#### #51/52
Similar to the #41/42, this route also circles Venice, but heads out to the Lido (rather than Murano) at the easternmost end of the circle. The #51 runs anticlockwise, the #52 clockwise, and both run fast through the Giudecca canal, stopping only at Záttere and Santa Marta between San Zaccaria and Piazzale Roma. Both run every 20min for most of the day. From 4.30–6am & 8.30–11pm the #51 doesn't do a complete lap of the city – instead it departs every 20 min from Fondamenta Nove and proceeds via the train station to the Lido, where it terminates; similarly, from 7–11pm the #52 (which starts operating at 6am) shuttles between the Lido and Fondamente Nove in the opposite direction, and from 11pm to around 1.30am goes no farther than the train station.

#### #LN
For most of the day the #Laguna Nord runs every half-hour from Fondamente Nove (hourly early in the morning and evenings), calling first at Murano-Faro before heading on to Mazzorbo, Burano (from where there is a connecting half-hourly #T shuttle to Torcello), Treporti and the Lido.

#### #N
This night service (11.30pm–4.30am) is a selective fusion of the #1 and #82 routes, running from the Lido to Giardini, San Zaccaria, San Marco (Vallaresso), Canal Grande (Accademia, San Samuele, San Tomà, Rialto, Ca' d'Oro, San Stae, San Marcuola), train station, Piazzale Roma, Tronchetto, Sacca Fisola, San Basilio, Záttere, Giudecca (Palanca, Redentore and Zitelle), San Giorgio and San Zaccaria, then retracing its route. It runs along the whole of the route in both directions roughly every 30min, and along the Rialto to Tronchetto part every 20min. Another night service connects Venice with Murano and Burano, running to and from Fondamente Nove every 30min between midnight and 4am.

## Traghetti

Costing just 40cents, **traghetti** (gondola ferries) are the only cheap way of getting a ride on a gondola, albeit a stripped-down version, with none of the trimmings and no padded seats – it's *de rigueur* to stand in the traghetto gondolas. The gondola traghetti across the Canal Grande are as follows; in the **winter** months it's common for traghetti services to be suspended.

**Santa Maria del Giglio–Salute**
(Mon–Sat 9am–7pm)

**Ca' Rezzonico–San Samuele**
(Mon–Sat 7.40am–1.20pm)

**San Tomà–Santo Stefano**
(Mon–Sat 7am–8.50pm, Sun 8am–7.50pm)

**Riva del Carbon–Riva del Vin**
(near Rialto, Mon–Sat 8am–2pm)

**Santa Sofia–Rialto**
(Mon–Sat 7am–8.50pm, Sun 8am–7.50pm)

**San Marcuola–Fondaco dei Turchi**
(Mon–Sat 7.30am–1.30pm)

In addition to these, some vaporetti and motoscafi operate as traghetti: for example, if you want to go from San Zaccaria over to San Giorgio Maggiore, or from one bank of the Canal Grande to the bank immediately opposite, you need only pay the lower traghetto fare of €1.80. If your journey is a short single-stop trip across a body of water, a traghetto fare almost certainly applies, even if it's not shown on the tariff list on the ticket booth.

## Gondolas

The **gondola** is the city's biggest cliché, but it's an astonishingly graceful craft, perfectly designed for negotiating the tortuous canals, and an hour's slow voyage through the city can give you a wholly new perspective on the place. To hire one costs €62 per fifty minutes for up to six passengers, rising to €77.45 between 8pm and 8am; you pay an extra €31 for every additional 25 minutes, or €38.75 from 8pm to 8am. Further hefty surcharges will be levied should you require the services of an on-board accordionist or tenor. Even though the tariff is set by the local authorities (and has stayed the same since 1997, so a rise must be imminent), it's been known for some gondoliers to try to extort even higher rates – if you do decide to go for a ride, establish the charge before setting off.

## Taxis

Venice's **water-taxis** are sleek and speedy vehicles that can penetrate all but the shallowest of the city's canals. Unfortunately their use is confined to all but the owners of the deepest pockets, for they are possibly the most expensive form of taxi in western Europe: the clock starts at €8.70 and goes up €1.30 every minute. All sorts of additional surcharges are levied as well – €1.60 for each extra person if there are more than four people in the party; €1.50 for each piece of luggage over 50cm long; €5.50 for a ride between 10pm and 7am. There are three ways of getting a taxi: go to one of the main stands (in front of the Piazzetta and at the airport), find one in the process of disgorging its passengers, or call one by phone (☎041.522.2303 or 041.723.112). If you phone for one, you'll pay a surcharge of €6.

# Museums and monuments

In an attempt to make sure that tourists go to see more than just the big central monuments, the city has introduced a number of combined tickets called **Museum Card**s. The card for **I Musei di Piazza San Marco**, costing €11 (€5.50 for EU students aged 15–29, EU citizens over 65 & Rolling Venice Card holders, €3 for children aged 6–14), allows you to visit the Palazzo Ducale, Museo Correr, Museo Archeologico and the Biblioteca Marciana. The **Area del Settecento** card (Museums of Eighteenth-Century Culture) covers Ca' Rezzonico, Casa Goldoni and the Palazzo Mocenigo, and costs €8/€4.50, while **I Musei delle Isole** (Island Museums) covers the Museo del Merletto (Burano) and the Museo del Vetro (Murano), and costs €6/€4. In addition to these, the **Museum Pass**, costing €15.50/€10, covers all the museums listed above. Cards are valid for three months,

allow one visit to each attraction, and are available from any of the participating museums. The **Musei di Piazza San Marco** can only be visited with a Museum Card; at the other places you have the option of paying an entry charge just for that attraction. The Internet site for all the museums mentioned above is ⓦwww.museicivicivenezliani.it. Note also the orange version of the Venice Card (see p.168) covers all of the museums covered by the Museum Pass.

Fourteen churches are now part of the **Chorus Pass** scheme (ⓦwww.chorusve.org), whereby an €8 ticket (€5 for holders of orange Venice Card) allows one visit to each of the churches over a one-year period. The individual entrance fee at each of the participating churches is €2, and all the churches (except for the Frari) observe the same opening hours: Monday to Saturday 10am to 5pm, Sunday 1 to 5pm (but closed Sunday in July and August). The churches involved are: Santa Maria del Giglio, Santo Stefano, Santa Maria Formosa; Santa Maria dei Miracoli, the Frari (all year Mon–Sat 9am–6pm, Sun 1–6pm), San Polo, San Giacomo dell'Orio, San Stae, Sant'Alvise, Madonna dell'Orto, San Pietro di Castello, Redentore, San Sebastiano and San Giovanni Elemosinario. The Chorus Pass is available at all of these churches, but the Frari doesn't issue the discounted version.

# Festivals and special events

As recently as just one generation ago Venice was a night city, where the residents of each parish set out tables on the street at the flimsiest excuse. Nowadays, with the pavements overrun by outsiders, the social life of the Venetians is more of an indoor business – a restaurant meal or a drink with friends might feature in most people's diary for the week, and a conversational stroll is certainly a favourite Venetian pastime, but home entertainment takes up most time and energy. That said, Venice's calendar of special events is pretty impressive, with the Carnevale, the Film Festival and the Biennale ranking among the continent's hottest dates. To find out **what's on** in the way of concerts and films, check *Un Ospite di Venezia*, a free bilingual magazine available from the tourist office and some of the more expensive hotels – it's produced weekly in peak season, monthly in winter. Information and listings for bars, events, festivals can also be found at ⓦ**www .govenice.com**.

## The Film Festival

The **Venice Film Festival**, founded in 1932, is the world's oldest and the most important in Europe after Cannes. The eleven-day event takes place on the Lido every year in **late August and/or early September**. Posters advertising the Festival's schedule appear weeks in advance, and the tourist office will have the Festival programme a fair time before the event, as will the two cinemas where the films are shown – the **Palazzo del Cinemà** on Lungomare G. Marconi and the neighbouring **PalaGalileo**. Tickets are available to the general public, but you have to go along and queue for them at the Pala-Galileo on the day before the performance. Any remaining tickets are sold off at PalaGalileo one hour before the screening, but nearly all shows are sold out well before then.

## The Biennale

The **Venice Biennale**, Europe's most glamorous international forum for contemporary art, was first held in 1895 as the city's contribution to the celebrations for the silver wedding anniversary of King Umberto I and Margherita of Savoy, and is now held **every odd-numbered year from June to November**. The main site is in the Giardini Pubblici, where there are permanent pavilions for about forty countries plus space for a thematic international exhibition. This central part of the Biennale is supplemented by exhibitions in larger venues all over the city, such as the salt warehouses on the Zàttere or the colossal Corderie. In addition, smaller sites throughout the city – including the streets and parks – host fringe exhibitions, installations and performances, particularly in the opening weeks. Some pavilions and other venues are used in non-Biennale years for an independent Biennale for **architecture**.

Information on the Biennale is available at Ⓦwww.labiennale.com.

# Carnevale

John Evelyn wrote of the 1646 Carnevale: "all the world was in Venice to see the folly and madness . . . the women, men and persons of all conditions disguising themselves in antique dresses, & extravagant Musique & a thousand gambols." Not much is different in today's Carnevale, for which people arrive in such numbers that the causeway from the mainland has sometimes had to be closed because the city has been too packed. Carnevale takes place over the **ten days leading up to Lent**, finishing on Shrove Tuesday with a masked ball for the glitterati, and dancing in the Piazza for the plebs. During the day people don costumes and go down to the Piazza to be photographed; parents dress up their kids; businessmen can be seen doing their shopping in the classic white mask, black cloak and tricorne hat. In the evening some congregate in the remoter squares, while those who have spent hundreds of euros on their costumes install themselves in the windows of *Florian's* and pose for a while. But you don't need to spend money or try to be "traditional" in your disguise: a simple black outfit and a painted face is enough to transform you from a spectator into a participant.

# La Sensa and Vogalonga

The feast of **La Sensa** happens in May on the **Sunday after Ascension Day** – the latter being the day on which the doge enacted the wedding of Venice to the sea. The ritual has recently been revived – a distinctly feeble procession which ends with the mayor and a gang of other dignitaries getting into a present-day approximation of the *Bucintoro* (the state barge) and sailing off to the Lido. A gondola regatta follows the ceremony, but far more spectacular is the **Vogalonga** (long row), which is held on the same day. Established in 1974 as a protest against the excessive number of motorboats on the canals, the *Vogalonga* is now open to any crew in any class of rowing boat, and covers a 32-kilometre course from the Bacino di San Marco out to Burano and back; the competitors set off at 8.30am and arrive at the bottom of the Canal Grande anywhere between about 11am and 3pm.

# Festa del Redentore

The **Festa del Redentore** is one of Venice's plague-related festivals, marking the end of the epidemic of 1576. Celebrated on the **third Sunday in July**, the day is centred on Palladio's church of the Redentore, which was built by way of thanksgiving for the city's escape. A bridge of boats is strung across the Giudecca canal to allow the faithful to walk over to the church, and on the Saturday night hundreds of people row out for a picnic on the water. The night ends with a grand fireworks display, after which it's traditional to row to the Lido for the sunrise.

# The Regata Storica

Held on the **first Sunday in September**, the **Regata Storica** is the annual trial of strength and skill for the city's gondoliers and other expert rowers. It starts with a procession of richly decorated historic craft along the Canal Grande course, their crews all decked out in period dress, followed by a series of races right up the canal. Re-enacting the return of Caterina Cornaro to her native city in 1489 (see p.65), the opening parade is a spectacular affair, and the races attract a sizeable (and partisan) crowd. The first race of the day is for young rowers in two-oared *pupparini*; the women's race comes next, and then it's the big one – the men's race, in specialized racing gondolas called *gondolini*.

# La Salute

Named after the church of the Salute, the **Festa della Salute** is a reminder of the plague of 1630–31, which killed one-third of the population of the lagoon.

The church was built in thanks for deliverance from the outbreak, and every **November 21** since then the Venetians have processed over a pontoon bridge across the Canal Grande to give thanks for their good health, or to pray for sick friends and relatives. It offers the only chance to see the church as it was designed to be seen – with its main doors open and hundreds of people milling up and down the steps.

# Directory

**ACTV ENQUIRIES** Piazzale Roma, daily 7.30am–8pm (☎041.528.7886); English-language information from Hello Venezia on ☎041.2424 (7.30am–8pm daily) or ⬤www.hellovenezia.it.

**AIRPORT ENQUIRIES** Marco Polo airport, ☎041.260.9260, ⬤www.veniceairport.it.

**AMERICAN EXPRESS** The American Express office is at Salizzada S. Moisè, San Marco 1471, a couple of minutes' walk west of the Piazza (Mon–Fri 9am–5.30pm, Sat 9am–12.30pm; ☎041.520.0844). Their emergency number is ☎800.64.046 (toll-free).

**BANKS** Banks in Venice are concentrated on Calle Larga XXII Marzo (west of the Piazza), and along the chain of squares and alleyways between Campo S. Bartolomeo and Campo Manin (in the north of the San Marco sestiere). There's not much to choose between them in terms of commission and exchange rates, and their hours are generally Mon–Fri 8.30am–1.30pm and 2.30–3.30pm. The main ones are as follows: **Banca Commerciale Italiana**, Calle Larga XXII Marzo, San Marco 2188; **Banca d'Italia**, Campo S. Bartolomeo, San Marco 4799; **Banca Credito Italiano**, Campo S. Salvador, San Marco; **Banco di Roma**, Mercerie dell'Orologio, San Marco 191; **Banco San Marco**, Calle Larga XXII Marzo, San Marco 383.

**CONSULATES AND EMBASSIES** The **British** consulate is in the Palazzo Querini, Dorsoduro 1051 ☎041.522.7207 (by the Accademia); this office is staffed by an honorary consul – the closest full consulate is in Milan, at Via San Paolo 7 ☎02.723.001. The nearest **US** consulate is also in Milan, at Via Principe Amedeo ☎02.290.351. Travellers from **Ireland**, **Australia**, **New Zealand** and **Canada** should contact their Rome embassies: Irish Embassy, Piazza di Campitelli 3 ☎06.697.9121; Australian Embassy, Via Alessandria 215 ☎041.06/852.721; New Zealand Embassy, Via Zara 28 ☎06.441.7171; Canadian Embassy, Via G. B. de Rossi 27 ☎041.06/445.981.

**EMERGENCIES** For all emergency services ring ☎113. Alternatively, dialling ☎112 puts you straight through to the *Carabinieri* (police), ☎115 goes straight to the *Vigili del Fuoco* (fire brigade) and ☎118 straight to *Pronto Soccorso Medico* (ambulance).

**EXCHANGE** There are clusters of exchange bureaux (*cambios*) where most tourists gather – near San Marco, the Rialto and the train station. Open late every day of the week, they can be useful in emergencies, but their rates of commission and exchange tend to be steep. The best rates are at American Express and the main banks.

**HOSPITAL** Ospedale Civile, Campo SS. Giovanni e Paolo; emergency department ☎041.529.4516.

**INTERNET ACCESS** Dozens of dedicated Internet points have opened in the last few years, and you'll also find them in numerous cafés and shops. Most charge €3–5 per half-hour, though rates usually drop the longer you stay online.

**LOST PROPERTY** If you lose anything on the train or at the station, call ☎041.785.238; at the airport call ☎041.260.6436; on the vaporetti call ☎041.272.2179, on the buses call ☎041.272.2838; and anywhere in the city itself call the town hall on ☎041.274.8225.

**POLICE** To notify police of a theft or lost passport, report to the *Questura* on Fondamenta S. Lorenzo (☎041.528.4666); in the event of an emergency, ring ☎113.

**POST OFFICES** Venice's main post office is in the Fondaco dei Tedeschi, near the Rialto bridge (Mon–Sat 8.30am–6.30pm). Any poste restante should be addressed to Fermo Posta, Fondaco dei Tedeschi, 80100 Venezia; take your passport along when collecting your post. The principal branch post offices are in Calle dell'Ascensione (Mon–Sat 8.10am–6pm) and at Záttere 1406 (same hours). Stamps can also be bought in *tabacchi*, as well as in some gift shops.

**PUBLIC TOILETS** The lack of public toilets in Venice used to be a common complaint from tourists, but AmaV (*Azienda multiservizi ambientale Veneziana*) has now installed facilities on or very near to most of the main squares, and all over the city you'll see green, blue and white AmaV signs high on the walls, directing you to the nearest public toilet. You'll need a 50cent coin, but the toilets are usually staffed, so you can get change; note that the Venice Card (see p.168) gives free access to all staffed AmaV toilets. The main facilities are at the train station, at Piazzale Roma, on the west side of the Accademia bridge, by the main tourist office at the Giardinetti Reali, off the west side of the Piazza, off Campo S. Bartolomeo, on Campo S. Polo, Campo Rialto Nuovo, Campo S. Leonardo, Campo San'Angelo and on Campo S. Margherita. Toilets are to be found in most of the city's bars as well; it's diplomatic, to say the least, to buy a drink before availing yourself.

**TELEPHONES** Nearly all Venice's public call-boxes accept nothing but phone cards, which can be bought from *tabacchi* and some other shops (look for the Telecom Italia sticker); the less expensive type of cards can be bought from machines by the Telecom Italia phone booths in Strada Nova (near S. Felice), Calle S. Luca, Piazzale Roma and adjoining the main post office building near the Rialto bridge. You're never far from a pay phone – every sizeable campo has at least one, and there are phones by every vaporetto stop.

# Language

# The basics

What follows is a brief pronunciation guide and a run-down of essential words and phrases. For more detail, get *Italian: A Rough Guide Dictionary Phrase Book*, which has a huge but accessible vocabulary, a detailed menu reader and useful dialogues.

## Pronunciation

Italian **pronunciation** is easy, since every word is spoken exactly as it's written. The only difficulties you're likely to encounter are the few **consonants** that are different from English:

**c** before **e** or **i** is pronounced as in **ch**urch, while **ch** before the same vowels is hard, as in **c**at.

**sci** or **sce** are pronounced as in **sh**eet and **sh**elter respectively.

**g** is soft before **e** and **i**, as in **g**eranium; hard when followed by **h**, as in **g**arlic.

**gn** has the ni sound of our "o**ni**on".

**gl** in Italian is softened to something like li in English, as in sta**ll**ion.

**h** is not aspirated, as in **h**onour.

All Italian words are **stressed** on the penultimate syllable unless an **accent** (´ or `) denotes otherwise, although written accents are often left out in practice. Note that the ending **–ia** or **–ie** counts as two syllables, hence trattoria is stressed on the **i**.

## Words and phrases

### Basic words and phrases

| | |
|---|---|
| **Good morning** | Buon giorno |
| **Good afternoon/ evening** | Buona sera |
| **Good night** | Buona notte |
| **Goodbye** | Arrivederci |
| **Yes** | Sì |
| **No** | No |
| **Please** | Per favore |
| **Thank you (very much)** | Grázie (molte/mille grazie) |
| **You're welcome** | Prego |
| **Alright/that's OK** | Va bene |
| **How are you?** | Come stai/sta? (informal/formal) |
| **I'm fine** | Bene |
| **Do you speak English?** | Parla inglese? |
| **I don't understand** | Non ho capito |
| **I don't know** | Non lo so |
| **Excuse me** | Mi scusi/Prego |
| **Excuse me (in a crowd)** | Permesso |
| **I'm sorry** | Mi dispiace |
| **I'm English** | Sono inglese |
| **Scottish** | scozzese |
| **American** | americano |
| **Irish** | irlandese |
| **Welsh** | gallese |
| **Today** | Oggi |
| **Tomorrow** | Domani |
| **Day after tomorrow** | Dopodomani |
| **Yesterday** | Ieri |
| **Now** | Adesso |
| **Later** | Più tardi |
| **Wait a minute!** | Aspetta! |
| **In the morning** | Di mattina |
| **In the afternoon** | Nel pomeriggio |
| **In the evening** | Di sera |
| **Here/there** | Qui/La |
| **Good/bad** | Buono/Cattivo |
| **Big/small** | Grande/Piccolo |
| **Cheap/expensive** | Económico/Caro |

| Hot/cold | Caldo/Freddo |
|---|---|
| Near/far | Vicino/Lontano |
| Vacant/occupied | Libero/Occupato |
| With/without | Con/Senza |
| More/less | Più/Meno |
| Enough, no more | Basta |
| Mr . . . | Signor . . . |
| Mrs . . . | Signora . . . |
| Miss . . . | Signorina . . . |
| | (il Signor, la Signora, la Signorina when speaking about someone else) |

## Numbers

| 1 | uno |
|---|---|
| 2 | due |
| 3 | tre |
| 4 | quattro |
| 5 | cinque |
| 6 | sei |
| 7 | sette |
| 8 | otto |
| 9 | nove |
| 10 | dieci |
| 11 | undici |
| 12 | dodici |
| 13 | tredici |
| 14 | quattordici |
| 15 | quindici |
| 16 | sedici |
| 17 | diciassette |
| 18 | diciotto |
| 19 | diciannove |
| 20 | venti |
| 21 | ventuno |
| 22 | ventidue |
| 30 | trenta |
| 40 | quaranta |
| 50 | cinquanta |
| 60 | sessanta |
| 70 | settanta |
| 80 | ottanta |
| 90 | novanta |
| 100 | cento |
| 101 | centuno |
| 110 | centodieci |
| 200 | duecento |
| 500 | cinquecento |
| 1000 | mille |
| 5000 | cinquemila |
| 10,000 | diecimila |
| 50,000 | cinquantamila |

## Some signs

| Entrance/exit | Entrata/Uscita |
|---|---|
| Open/closed | Aperto/Chiuso |
| Arrivals/departures | Arrivi/Partenze |
| Closed for restoration | Chiuso per restauro |
| Closed for holidays | Chiuso per ferie |
| Pull/push | Tirare/Spingere |
| Do not touch | Non toccare |
| Danger | Perícolo |
| Beware | Attenzione |
| First aid | Pronto soccorso |
| Ring the bell | Suonare il campanello |
| No smoking | Vietato fumare |

## Transport

| Ferry | Traghetto |
|---|---|
| Bus station | Autostazione |
| Train station | Stazione ferroviaria |
| A ticket to . . . | Un biglietto a . . . |
| One-way/return | Solo andata/ andata e ritorno |
| What time does it leave? | A che ora parte? |
| Where does it leave from? | Da dove parte? |

## Accommodation

| Hotel | Albergo |
|---|---|
| Do you have a room . . . | Ha una cámera . . . |
| for one/two/three people | per una/due/tre person(a/e) |
| for one/two/three nights | per una/due/tre nott(e/i) |
| for one/two weeks | per una/due settiman(a/e) |
| with a double bed | con un letto matrimoniale |
| with a shower/ bath | con una doccia/ un bagno |
| How much is it? | Quanto costa? |
| Is breakfast included? | È compresa la prima colazione? |
| Do you have anything cheaper? | Ha niente che costa di meno? |
| I'll take it | La prendo |
| I'd like to book a room | Vorrei prenotare una cámera |
| I have a booking | Ho una prenotazione |
| Youth hostel | Ostello per la gioventù |

### Questions and directions

| | |
|---|---|
| Where? | Dove? |
| (where is/are . . ?) | (Dov'è/Dove sono) |
| When? | Quando? |
| What? (what is it?) | Cosa? (Cos'è?) |
| How much/many? | Quanto/Quanti? |
| Why? | Perché? |
| It is/there is | È/C'è |
| (is it/is there . . ?) | (È/C'è . . . ?) |
| What time is it? | Che ora è/ |
| | Che ore sono? |

| | |
|---|---|
| How do I get to . . ? | Come arrivo a . . ? |
| What time does it open? | A che ora apre? |
| What time does it close? | A che ora chiude? |
| How much does it cost ? | Quanto costa? |
| ( . . do they cost?) | (Quanto cóstano?) |
| What's it called in Italian? | Come si chiama in italiano? |

# Menu reader

This glossary should allow you to decode most menus; it concludes with a summary of Venetian specialities.

### Basics and snacks

| | |
|---|---|
| Aceto | Vinegar |
| Aglio | Garlic |
| Biscotti | Biscuits |
| Burro | Butter |
| Caramelle | Sweets |
| Cioccolato | Chocolate |
| Focaccia | Oven-baked bread-based snack |
| Formaggio | Cheese |
| Frittata | Omelette |
| Gelato | Ice cream |
| Grissini | Bread sticks |
| Marmellata | Jam |
| Olio | Oil |
| Olive | Olives |
| Pane | Bread |
| Pane integrale | Wholemeal bread |
| Panino | Bread roll |
| Patatine | Crisps |
| Patatine fritte | Chips |
| Pepe | Pepper |
| Pizzetta | Small cheese-and-tomato pizza |
| Riso | Rice |
| Sale | Salt |
| Tramezzini | Sandwich |
| Uova | Eggs |
| Yogurt | Yoghurt |
| Zúcchero | Sugar |
| Zuppa | Soup |

### Starters (Antipasti)

| | |
|---|---|
| Antipasto misto | Mixed cold meats and cheese (and a selection of other things in this list) |
| Caponata | Mixed aubergine, olives, tomatoes and celery |
| Caprese | Tomato and mozzarella salad |
| Insalata di mare | Seafood salad |
| Insalata di riso | Rice salad |
| Melanzane in parmigiana | Fried aubergine in tomato and parmesan cheese |
| Mortadella | Salami-type cured meat |

| | |
|---|---|
| Pancetta | Bacon |
| Peperonata | Grilled green, red or yellow peppers stewed in olive oil |
| Pomodori ripieni | Stuffed tomatoes |
| Prosciutto | Ham |
| Salame | Salami |

## Soups

| | |
|---|---|
| Brodo | Clear broth |
| Minestrina | Any light soup |
| Minestrone | Thick vegetable soup |
| Pasta e fagioli | Pasta soup with beans |
| Pastina in brodo | Pasta pieces in clear broth |
| Stracciatella | Broth with egg |

## Pasta

| | |
|---|---|
| Cannelloni | Large tubes of pasta, stuffed |
| Farfalle | Literally "bow"-shaped pasta; the word also means "butterflies" |
| Fettuccine | Narrow pasta ribbons |
| Gnocchi | Small potato and dough dumplings |
| Lasagne | Lasagne |
| Maccheroni | Tubular spaghetti |
| Pasta al forno | Pasta baked with minced meat, eggs, tomato and cheese |
| Penne | Smaller version of rigatoni |
| Ravioli | Small packets of stuffed pasta |
| Rigatoni | Large, grooved tubular pasta |
| Risotto | Cooked rice dish, with sauce |
| Spaghetti | Spaghetti |
| Spaghettini | Thin spaghetti |
| Tagliatelle | Pasta ribbons, another word for fettuccine |
| Tortellini | Small rings of pasta, stuffed with meat or cheese |
| Vermicelli | Very thin spaghetti (literally "little worms") |

## Pasta sauces

| | |
|---|---|
| Aglio e olio | Tossed in garlic and olive oil |
| (e peperoncino) | (and hot chillies) |
| Arrabbiata | Spicy tomato sauce |
| Bolognese | Meat sauce |
| Burro e salvia | Butter and sage |
| Carbonara | Cream, ham and beaten egg |
| Frutta di mare | Seafood |
| Funghi | Mushroom |
| Matriciana | Cubed pork and tomato sauce |
| Panna | Cream |
| Parmigiano | Parmesan cheese |
| Pesto | Ground basil, pine nut, garlic and pecorino sauce |
| Pomodoro | Tomato sauce |
| Ragù | Meat sauce |
| Vóngole | Clam and tomato sauce |

## Meat (carne)

| | |
|---|---|
| Agnello | Lamb |
| Bistecca | Steak |
| Coniglio | Rabbit |
| Costolette | Chops |
| Cotolette | Cutlets |
| Fegatini | Chicken livers |
| Fégato | Liver |
| Involtini | Steak slices, rolled and stuffed |
| Lingua | Tongue |
| Maiale | Pork |
| Manzo | Beef |
| Ossobuco | Shin of veal |
| Pollo | Chicken |
| Polpette | Meatballs (or balls of anything minced) |
| Rognoni | Kidneys |
| Salsiccia | Sausage |
| Saltimbocca | Veal with ham |
| Spezzatino | Stew |
| Tacchino | Turkey |
| Trippa | Tripe |
| Vitello | Veal |

## Fish (pesce) and shellfish (crostacei)

| | |
|---|---|
| Acciughe | Anchovies |
| Anguilla | Eel |
| Aragosta | Lobster |
| Baccalà | Dried salted cod |
| Bronzino/ Branzino | Sea-bass |
| Calamari | Squid |
| Cape lungue | Razor clams |
| Cape sante | Scallops |
| Caparossoli | Shrimps |

| | |
|---|---|
| Coda di rospo | Monkfish |
| Cozze | Mussels |
| Dentice | Dentex (like sea bass) |
| Gamberetti | Shrimps |
| Gámberi | Prawns |
| Granchio | Crab |
| Merluzzo | Cod |
| Orata | Bream |
| Ostriche | Oysters |
| Pescespada | Swordfish |
| Pólipo | Octopus |
| Ricci di mare | Sea urchins |
| Rombo | Turbot |
| San Pietro | John Dory |
| Sarde | Sardines |
| Schie | Shrimps |
| Seppie | Cuttlefish |
| Sógliola | Sole |
| Tonno | Tuna |
| Triglie | Red mullet |
| Trota | Trout |
| Vóngole | Clams |

## Vegetables (contorni) and salad (insalata)

| | |
|---|---|
| Asparagi | Asparagus |
| Basílico | Basil |
| Bróccoli | Broccoli |
| Cápperi | Capers |
| Carciofi | Artichokes |
| Carciofini | Artichoke hearts |
| Carotte | Carrots |
| Cavolfiori | Cauliflower |
| Cávolo | Cabbage |
| Ceci | Chickpeas |
| Cetriolo | Cucumber |
| Cipolla | Onion |
| Fagioli | Beans |
| Fagiolini | Green beans |
| Finocchio | Fennel |
| Funghi | Mushrooms |
| Insalata verde/ | Green salad/ |
| insalata mista | mixed salad |
| Melanzana | Aubergine/eggplant |
| Orígano | Oregano |
| Patate | Potatoes |
| Peperoni | Peppers |
| Piselli | Peas |
| Pomodori | Tomatoes |
| Radicchio | Chicory |
| Spinaci | Spinach |
| Zucchini | Courgettes |
| Zucca | Pumpkin |

## Desserts (dolci)

| | |
|---|---|
| Amaretti | Macaroons |
| Cassata | Ice-cream cake with candied fruit |
| Gelato | Ice cream |
| Macedonia | Fruit salad |
| Torta | Cake, tart |
| Zabaglione | Dessert made with eggs, sugar and Marsala wine |
| Zuppa Inglese | Trifle |

## Cheese (formaggi)

| | |
|---|---|
| Caciocavallo | A type of dried, mature mozzarella cheese |
| Fontina | Northern Italian cheese used in cooking |
| Gorgonzola | Soft blue-veined cheese |
| Mozzarella | Bland soft white cheese used on pizzas |
| Parmigiano | Parmesan cheese |
| Pecorino | Strong-tasting hard sheep's cheese |
| Provolone | Hard strong cheese |
| Ricotta | Soft white cheese made from ewe's milk, used in sweet or savoury dishes |

## Fruit (frutta) and nuts (noce)

| | |
|---|---|
| Ananas | Pineapple |
| Anguria/ Coccómero | Watermelon |
| Arance | Oranges |
| Banane | Bananas |
| Ciliegie | Cherries |
| Fichi | Figs |
| Fichi d'India | Prickly pears |
| Frágole | Strawberries |
| Limone | Lemon |
| Mándorle | Almonds |
| Mele | Apples |
| Melone | Melon |
| Pere | Pears |
| Pesche | Peaches |
| Pignoli | Pine nuts |
| Pistacchio | Pistachio nut |
| Uva | Grapes |

## Drinks

| | |
|---|---|
| Acqua minerale | Mineral water |
| Aranciata | Orangeade |

| | |
|---|---|
| Bicchiere | Glass |
| Birra | Beer |
| Bottiglia | Bottle |
| Caffè | Coffee |
| Cioccolata calda | Hot chocolate |
| Ghiaccio | Ice |
| Granita | Iced coffee or fruit drink |
| Latte | Milk |
| Limonata | Lemonade |
| Selz | Soda water |
| Spremuta | Fresh fruit juice |
| Spumante | Sparkling wine |
| Succo | Concentrated fruit juice with sugar |
| Tè | Tea |
| Tónico | Tonic water |
| Vino | Wine |
| Rosso | Red |
| Bianco | White |
| Rosato | Rosé |
| Secco | Dry |
| Dolce | Sweet |
| Litro | Litre |
| Mezzo | Half |
| Quarto | Quarter |
| Salute! | Cheers! |

# Venetian specialities

## Antipasti (starters) e Primi (first course)

| | |
|---|---|
| Acciughe marinate | Marinated anchovies with onions |
| Bigoli in salsa | Spaghetti with butter, onions and sardines |
| Brodetto | Mixed fish soup, often with tomatoes and garlic |
| Castraura | Artichoke hearts |
| Granseola alla Veneziana | Crab cooked with oil, parsley and lemon |

| | |
|---|---|
| Pasta e fagioli | Pasta and beans |
| San Prosciutto Daniele | The best quality prosciutto |
| Risotto di mare | Mixed seafood risotto |
| Risotto di cape | Risotto with clams and shellfish |
| Risotto alla sbirraglia | Risotto with chicken, vegetables and ham |
| Risotto alla trevigiana | Risotto with butter, onions and chicory |
| Sopa de peoci | Mussel soup with garlic and parsley |

## Secondi (second course)

| | |
|---|---|
| Anguilla alla Veneziana | Eel cooked with lemon and tuna |
| Baccalà mantecato | Salt cod simmered in milk |
| Fegato veneziana | Sliced calf's liver cooked in olive oil with onion |
| Peoci salati | Mussels with parsley and garlic |
| Risi e bisi | Rice and peas, with parmesan and ham |
| Sarde in saor | Marinated sardines |
| Seppie in nero | Squid cooked in its ink |
| Seppioline nere | Baby cuttlefish cooked in its ink |

## Dolci

| | |
|---|---|
| Frittole alla Veneziana | Rum- and anise-flavoured fritters filled with pine nuts, raisins and candied fruit |
| Tiramisù | Dessert of layered chocolate and cream, flavoured with rum and coffee |

# Index and small print

## A Rough Guide to Rough Guides

Venice DIRECTIONS is published by Rough Guides. The first *Rough Guide to Greece*, published in 1982, was a student scheme that became a publishing phenomenon. The immediate success of the book – with numerous reprints and a Thomas Cook prize shortlisting – spawned a series that rapidly covered dozens of destinations. Rough Guides had a ready market among low-budget backpackers, but soon also acquired a much broader and older readership that relished Rough Guides' wit and inquisitiveness as much as their enthusiastic, critical approach. Everyone wants value for money, but not at any price. Rough Guides soon began supplementing the "rougher" information about hostels and low-budget listings with the kind of detail on restaurants and quality hotels that independent-minded visitors on any budget might expect, whether on business in New York or trekking in Thailand. These days the guides offer recommendations from shoestring to luxury and a large number of destinations around the globe, including almost every country in the Americas and Europe, more than half of Africa and most of Asia and Australasia. Rough Guides now publish:

- Travel guides to more than 200 worldwide destinations
- Dictionary phrasebooks to 22 major languages
- Maps printed on rip-proof and waterproof Polyart™ paper
- Music guides running the gamut from Opera to Elvis
- Reference books on topics as diverse as the Weather and Shakespeare
- World Music CDs in association with World Music Network

Visit **www.roughguides.com** to see our latest publications.

## Publishing Information

This 1st edition published May 2004 by **Rough Guides Ltd**, 80 Strand, London WC2R 0RL. 345 Hudson St, 4th Floor, New York, NY 10014, USA.

**Distributed by the Penguin Group**
Penguin Books Ltd, 80 Strand, London WC2R 0RL
Penguin Group (USA), 375 Hudson Street, NY 10014, USA
Penguin Group (Australia), 487 Maroondah Highway, PO Box 257, Ringwood, Victoria 3134, Australia
Penguin Group (Canada), 10 Alcorn Avenue, Toronto, Ontario, Canada M4V 1E4
Penguin Group (NZ), 182–190 Wairau Road, Auckland 10, New Zealand
Typeset in Bembo and Helvetica to an original design by Henry Iles.
Printed and bound in Italy by Graphicom

192pp includes index
A catalogue record for this book is available from the British Library

ISBN 1-84353-353-7

1  3  5  7  9  8  6  4  2

## Help us update

We've gone to a lot of effort to ensure that the first edition of **Venice DIRECTIONS** is accurate and up-to-date. However, things change – places get "discovered", opening hours are notoriously fickle, restaurants and rooms raise prices or lower standards. If you feel we've got it wrong or left something out, we'd like to know, and if you can remember the address, the price, the time, the phone number, so much the better.

We'll credit all contributions, and send a copy of the next edition (or any other DIRECTIONS guide or Rough Guide if you prefer) for the best letters. Everyone who writes to us and isn't already a subscriber will receive a copy of our full-colour thrice-yearly newsletter. Please mark letters: **"Venice DIRECTIONS Update"** and send to: Rough Guides, 80 Strand, London WC2R 0RL, or Rough Guides, 4th Floor, 345 Hudson St, New York, NY 10014. Or send an email to **mail@roughguides.com**

Have your questions answered and tell others about your trip at **www.roughguides.atinfopop.com**

## Rough Guide Credits

**Text editor**: Kate Berens
**Layout**: Andy Hilliard
**Photography**: Neil Setchfield
**Cartography**: Manish Chandra, Jai Prakash Mishra, Rajesh Chhibber, Ashutosh Bharti, Rajesh Mishra, Animesh Pathak

**Picture research**: Sharon Martins, Mark Thomas
**Proofreader**: Diane Margolis
**Production**: Julia Bovis
**Design**: Henry Iles

**SMALL PRINT**

## The author

Jonathan Buckley wrote the *Rough Guide to Venice*, is the co-author of *Rough Guides* to Tuscany & Umbria and Florence, and has published four novels: *The Biography of Thomas Lang*, *Xerxes*, *Ghost MacIndoe* and *Invisible*.

## Acknowledgements

Thanks to Charles Hebbert and Kate Hughes for updating; and to Katie Lloyd-Jones and Lucy Ratcliffe.

# Index

NOTES